"Deb is amazing! She is a gifted writer who has succeeded in drawing together the insights that successful women use to overcome challenges in today's complex world. Bravo!"

—JANET H. ADKINS
Supervisor of Elections, Nassau County, Florida

"What a gift Deb has given women in her latest book, *Women on Top*. Through her own and others' lived experiences, she shares valuable leadership lessons and advice for getting past the roadblocks that hold so many women back. It is a comprehensive guide for women of any age who aspire to lead."

—NANCY HOWELL AGEE
President and CEO, Carilion Clinic

"In this must-read book, you will learn to overcome your fears, take ownership of your success, and close the gap between *where you are* and *where you want to be*. Within this inspiring read, you learn that leadership and lipstick are not mutually exclusive.

"While there are more highly qualified women in the workforce today than ever before, most of us are not reaching our full potential when compared to our male counterparts. Motivational speaker and author Deb Boelkes decided to find out why. In *Women on Top,* she identifies the differences between those who get promoted to executive leadership and those who do not. She reveals what makes those on the leading edge tick and how you too can reach your own potential.

"Within these pages, you will learn lessons from relentless and fearless, yet caring, authentic, smart, feminine, and humble women at the top—whose experience ranges from business to the military. You will hear real-life stories about how even you can boost your potential to advance to the next level, no matter what career stage you are in.

"Most importantly, Deb speaks to both the self-inflicted and cultural forces that hold us back. She urges us to become more aware of how we may be holding ourselves back, and she encourages us to take risks, challenge ourselves, and pursue our goals with passion. In just fourteen chapters, you'll learn how to courageously navigate the forces shaping the modern workplace with authenticity—and in your high heels."

—DAWN LEOTA ALEXANDER, MBA
Certified Financial Planner™, Finance Executive

"YOU WILL NOT BE ABLE TO PUT THIS BOOK DOWN! In Deb's third book, *Women on Top: What's Keeping You from Executive Leadership?* readers will get an abundance of insights that are instrumental in empowering them to take tangible steps in their own leadership journey. It's a must-read for all female leaders and executives currently in leadership roles and for those women who are just starting their career and/or leadership journey. This book gets to the core of what is impeding women's growth and trajectory in executive leadership. There has been a dearth of testimonials and real-life examples of women who have gone before us and who have learned along the way—until now. This book can and should serve as an indispensable developmental resource for all women aspiring for more in executive leadership."

—KRISTIN STRAITER CAMPBELL, PHD
Executive Coach, Kristin Campbell Coaching

"Do you want to laugh? Do you want to see what authentic leadership looks like from the inside? Have you ever asked yourself, *How did those female CEOs do it?* If you answered yes to any of these questions, stop and read this book! This book is filled with excellent advice from remarkable women who have succeeded in achieving executive leadership. It is definitely worth your time to learn how other women have overcome the same struggles you are feeling and experiencing. The candid feedback and advice from women who have succeeded is refreshing and enlightening. I truly wish this existed when I was coming up through the leadership ranks."

—LIEUTENANT GENERAL KATHLEEN M. GAINEY
U.S. Army, Retired

"This insightful book is uniquely designed to provide rich content by intertwining stories from some of the most prominent women executives in business today. Deb Boelkes is an outstanding writer, and she has chosen the most relevant and timely topics for this book. I value and respect her perspectives and advice on leadership because she has 'walked the walk' in her life and career. The unexpected treasures in this book are the stories and the philosophies of the women executives Deb chose as contributors. I so wish I had all her books earlier in my life to serve as a guide and to soothe the loneliness that comes with executive management. This is much more than a book on leadership—it is an inspiration!"

—WENDY JOHNSON
Former President and CEO, Dale Carnegie franchise, Atlanta, Georgia

"Deb Boelkes is the ultimate authority on building the best leaders and best places to work. Deb's latest gift, *Women on Top*, is a must-read that addresses the obstacles in America's large organizations and provides a clear path to greater excellence. Deb expertly weaves interpersonal and workplace dynamics as seen through the eyes of exceptional leaders, like the amazing Lt. Gen. Kathleen M. Gainey. Deb's powerful questions and topic areas get to the heart of what matters most—how to free women to soar to the top and unleash everyone's talents to deliver extraordinary results."

—COLONEL DEBRA M. LEWIS
U.S. Army, Retired
Founder, Mentally Tough Women

"*Women on Top* is truly a must-read for every woman. Deb Boelkes gives us a road map that is at once powerful and riveting. Through stories and interviews, Deb shines a light through the lens that women use to view the business world—and it's a very different lens than men use!

"What will help women move to greater equality in leadership is seeing more clearly the world men see and transforming it with our humanness. We have so much to share with men that will make our world of business a more diverse and equitable place; we just need to find a path to do that with graciousness and wins on all sides.

"Settle in with a cuppa and enjoy the ride with Deb!"

—JERRI ROSEN
Founder and CEO, Working Wardrobes

"With insights and wisdom straight from the heart of C-suite women, *Women on Top: What's Keeping You from Executive Leadership?* describes the journey of how to become a woman on top. The straight-up, tell-it-like-it-is, real-life experiences shared create a dynamic picture of how the C-suite is evolving from traditional to transformational.

"You will get a candid, behind-the-curtain view of 'her-story.' The *introspections* and *reflection points* offer key takeaways and great reference points for aspiring women leaders. You'll deepen your engagement with each chapter.

"Praises for Deb Boelkes for inspiring WOW factor workplaces today and tomorrow's best-ever leaders in her book series. We are living in novel times with unique risks. There has never been a bigger reason for workplace well-being and leadership transformation."

—MICHELLE ST. JANE, LLB, MA (PHILANTHROPY)
PHD (STRATEGY & HUMAN RESOURCE MANAGEMENT)
Strategist for Compassionate Leaders, Video Podcaster, and eSpeaker

Women on Top

What's Keeping You From **Executive Leadership?**

Deb Boelkes

Author of **The WOW Factor Workplace**
and **Heartfelt Leadership**

Published by:
Business World Rising, LLC
businessworldrising.com

Library of Congress Control Number: 2021913822
ISBN trade paper: 978-1-7340761-6-5
ISBN eBook: 978-1-7340761-7-2
ISBN audio book: 978-1-7340761-8-9

Business | Leadership | Management | Career

First Edition
Printed in the USA

To my inspiration and nana, Olive;
and
To Shannon, the university student who asked,
"As a female in a male-dominated environment,
how can I stand out?"
May you be everything you want to be.

Contents

Introduction

*I know, deep inside, you already have what it
takes to succeed as the woman on top.*

-DEB BOELKES

What's keeping you from executive leadership?

In organizations the world over, there are about as many women as
men at the lowest levels of the career ladder. Yet, at each
successively higher level, the proportion of women steadily
shrinks. While forty-one of the Fortune 500 CEOs are women—a
record high—that's only 8.1 percent of the total. What's keeping
women from executive leadership?

According to *Women in the Workplace 2019*, a report compiled by
LeanIn.org and McKinsey & Company, "If first-level women
managers were hired and promoted like men, there would be one

million more women in management over the next five years." In 2020, the global consulting firm Mercer found just 23 percent of the executive-level positions in over 1,100 organizations across the world were held by women.

Meanwhile, a March 2021 report by McKinsey & Company found that working women were disproportionately impacted by the COVID-19 crisis: "The pandemic had a near-immediate effect on women's employment. One in four women are considering leaving the workforce or downshifting their careers versus one in five men." The article went on to cite three groups of women who experienced the largest challenges: black women, working mothers, and women in senior management positions.

Something is clearly keeping women from executive leadership. It's not just the pandemic—this event simply fanned the flames of a malady that was already there.

On a more positive note, women are making some inroads into political leadership. The United States has inaugurated its first female vice president. Sixteen percent of U.S. state governors and an impressive 44 percent of lieutenant governors are women. According to the National Conference of State Legislatures, the number of women serving in leadership roles within state legislatures—as speaker of the House, president of the Senate, speaker pro tem, Senate president pro tem, majority leader, or minority leader—reached an all-time high of ninety in 2021, a 50 percent increase in just five years. Likewise in 2021, women held a record one hundred eighteen seats in the U.S. House of

Representatives (27.1 percent), up almost 40 percent from five years ago. Women also hold twenty-four of the one hundred seats in the U.S. Senate, up 20 percent from five years ago.

I bring up the political statistics not to draw a sharp distinction between the private and public sectors (though it *is* interesting to note that in the past year of lockdowns, women seem to have fallen behind in the former while making headway in the latter) but to show that, in general, there appears to be a growing societal acceptance of women in positions of leadership. That's a huge positive. It seems external conditions are favorable for us to now ascend to the highest echelons of corporate America.

So, when you consider the relatively equal proportions of men to women in the overall workplace, why aren't more women advancing to executive leadership inside America's corporations?

This is especially perplexing when you consider that bringing out the best in others, something most women do instinctively, is one of the most important responsibilities of an executive-level leader. We excel at the so-called "soft skills"—like empathy, teamwork, relationship-building, communication, and so forth—that have become increasingly valued over the past few decades and will continue to be in demand in the future. Soft skills—which some men find the most difficult to master— are the foundation upon which "Best Place to Work" organizations are built.

Bringing out the best in others, something most women do instinctively, is one of the most important responsibilities of an executive-level leader.

Think about it. Women, in general, instinctively nurture and motivate others. As children, we nurture our pets and baby dolls. We nurture our siblings when they are down. As teenagers, we nurture our friends and encourage our team members. As mothers, we nurture and inspire our children to do their best. As we get older, we do whatever it takes to enable our aging parents to enjoy their golden years. For the most part, we women are naturally good at encouraging and nurturing most everyone we care about. Yet, for most women, promotions to executive leadership are not forthcoming. Why not?

If you are wondering what is keeping most women from executive leadership, this book will likely be quite an eye-opener. The answers may not be what you think. And I hope it will also be an impetus to seize the wealth of leadership opportunities that await, just there for the taking.

This Book Is for You—Yes, *You*

If you are a woman who is intrigued by the notion of someday leading an organization at the executive level, as the woman on top, this book is for you. This is true whether you are just beginning to explore career options; considering whether you should go to a trade school, college, or post-graduate school; trying to land a job you will love; positioning to win a promotion; or concerned you may have reached an insurmountable career plateau. The book is also for anyone parenting, managing, or mentoring a woman who may be pondering any of these issues.

Within these pages, you will find the kind of candid and insightful "been there, done that" advice that I and most of the ambitious career women I know—including those who have made it to the top—wish we could have had to help streamline our own journeys up the proverbial career ladder. This book is designed to provide you with the kind of "ah ha," demystifying mentorship that can accelerate your rise to a richly rewarding life in the executive suite.

Within this book—and its follow-on, *Strong Suit: Leadership Success Secrets from Women on Top*—I will share my own career lessons learned over the course of my twenty-five-plus years in Fortune 500 leadership. I will also share the insights I subsequently gained as an entrepreneur dedicated to the advancement of women to senior leadership. Moreover, you will hear directly from seven amazing women who ultimately made it to the top echelons of some of the most well-known and highly respected organizations in North America.

Knowing firsthand that we women can sometimes be our own worst enemies, I hope this book may serve as a much-needed wake-up call. It focuses on what you really need to know to get out of your own way. Together, we will explore a variety of challenging issues, like recognizing and dealing with gender bias, the importance of developing and delegating to others, the downsides of

We women can sometimes be our own worst enemies; I hope this book may serve as a much-needed wake-up call.

following too closely in the footsteps of a role model, the relevance

vi Women on Top

of post-secondary education in today's business world, overcoming self-inflicted hurdles, and a variety of other gotchas.

At the end of each chapter, you will find helpful reflections that synthesize salient takeaways. You will also find introspective questions, which I urge you to consider, as they can help you see yourself through new eyes. The purpose of these questions is to help you appreciate the fact that what you really need to know to succeed is already inside you. Therefore, these end-of-chapter questions are purposely designed to help you find your own hidden gems.

I began writing this book shortly after I founded my leadership development company in 2009, originally called Business Women Rising and now known as Business World Rising. But I quickly got sidetracked as we mentored more and more of our high-potential female clients and came to discover just how many of them believed that theirs were not such great places to work.

When some of them asked us pointblank, "Why would I want to lead a place like that?" and confided that they not only had no idea how to turn their ships around, but they were afraid to even try, we realized there was another problem that needed to be addressed first.

To successfully enable these women—or anyone—to become the kind of inspirational leaders they had the potential to be, we first needed to educate them on what a great place to work could be like. Hence, I wrote a different first book from the one I had originally planned. I called it *The WOW Factor Workplace: How to Create a Best Place to Work Culture.*

In that book, I shared my own corporate leadership experiences in creating the kinds of workplaces where the best and most talented people lined up to get in. Also, my business protégé, Mark Goulston, MD, and I interviewed and shared the firsthand insights of several exceptional, Best Place to Work award-winning leaders. In that book and its follow-up, each of the inspiring "best-ever bosses" highlighted share their all-too-uncommon leadership philosophies and success secrets.

In my second book, *Heartfelt Leadership: How to Capture the Top Spot and Keep on Soaring,* we tackled the myriad of issues that some leaders believe are the most difficult challenges they face. Moreover, those same award-winning leaders featured in the first book went on to reveal how they evolved into the truly inspirational leaders they ultimately became.

Essentially, that first two-book series established the foundation upon which aspiring leaders could build the kind of organizations that employees love to work for and to which customers are loyal. With that series published, I was then able to focus on the book(s) I had originally set out to write.

And so…here we are.

You're Reading My Grandmother's Legacy

Before we proceed to Chapter One, I want to share a very personal secret with you. My desire to write the book(s) you are now about to read sprouted long ago—out of a personal regret that I failed to interview my own beloved woman-on-top grandmother when she was still alive.

When I was a young girl, my nana would nonchalantly tell me little stories of how she worked in her father's hairdressing business, as a teenager in England during World War I. She spoke lovingly of how she came to marry a handsome American soldier and sailed off with him to a new life in California after the war. She shared snippets of what her life was like as a stay-at-home mom until the day her handsome young husband suddenly dropped dead of a heart attack. At that instant, just in her mid-thirties, she was left alone to raise a seven-year-old daughter. She had no choice but to take over running her husband's business, just to keep food on the table during the Depression and the Second World War.

When I heard those stories all those years ago, my childish assumption was that these were just the kinds of things all women do. I concluded that this was normal life for grown-ups. It never dawned on me just how difficult it must have been for her to suddenly have to step in to run a business as a single mom, at a time when few women did so.

I never once questioned how she managed to survive and succeed—not only as a single, working mother, but as the woman on top. It never struck me as at all unusual or incredible in any way, until she was gone. It was only after I embarked on my own adult career journey at age nineteen, that I grew curious about how on earth she did it. But by then it was too late for me to ask her. So, I was left wondering—and I still wonder, in awe and with great admiration, to this very day.

Now, as a grandmother myself to an armful of adorable young granddaughters, I know from experience it will probably be years before they might have such questions for me. I also realize that, like my own nana, I may not be around to share my own sage advice about how or why I did what I did during my own leadership career, when they are mature enough to wonder about such things. I also know this: I do not want these girls to ever regret not knowing the details of my "been there, done that" experience.

I do not want these girls to ever regret not knowing the details of my "been there, done that" experience.

So, to be honest with you, the real purpose of this *Women on Top* book series is to impart the best sage career advice currently available to every granddaughter, everywhere, wherever they may be along their own career journeys. My hope is that these books will help accelerate the advancement of all aspiring, high-potential granddaughters to senior leadership, and that they, in turn, will someday inspire the next generation of career-minded granddaughters as well.

When you finish reading this book, be sure to read the follow-on, *Strong Suit: Leadership Success Secrets from Women on Top*. In that book, we will dive deeper into the real-life lessons learned by the very same women you are about to come to know on an intimate basis here. You will hear each one lay out, in their own words, what worked and what did not work for them over the course of their careers. Together, we will cover important topics like juggling motherhood and career pursuits, capitalizing on one's strengths, the importance of mastering soft skills and the art of communication, developing relationships at the top, learning from failure, and much more.

Armed with all the knowledge you are about to gain from this series, I expect you will be inspired to give it all you have got. You will have no more excuses or desire to blame others, because you will have finally garnered the insights and confidence needed to maximize your potential. And when you look at the big picture, I hope you'll see that you, along with other bright, talented, ambitious, and optimistic women, are perfectly positioned to rise to amazing new heights.

I know, deep inside, you already have what it takes to succeed as the woman on top. So read on—and don't let anything keep you from executive leadership.

-DEB BOELKES

ONE

The Great Awakening

Women helping each other—coaching,
mentoring, and providing tips—is a
great way for us to be our own force.

-INDRA NOOYI
Former Chairperson and Chief Executive Officer, PepsiCo

here did all the women go? I thought as I stood confidently at the head of the boardroom conference table, acknowledging my all-male audience.

Just minutes before, the executive assistant to the chief executive officer, a professionally dressed middle-aged woman, had escorted me upstairs from the lobby to lead the day's briefing.

At the time, I was head of Arrow Electronics' software-as-a-service organization. It was my responsibility to ensure our North American-based technology manufacturing clients understood the legal ramifications of a recently adopted directive of the European Union (EU) regarding the Restriction of Hazardous Substances

(RoHS) in electrical and electronic equipment. Non-compliance with this directive could have potentially led to financial disaster for companies that sold electrical or electronic products into the EU. My goal this day was to help our customers mitigate that risk.

As the CEO's executive assistant placed a glass of water on the crystal coaster in front of me, she asked, "Is there anything else I can get for you?"

I scanned the richly paneled room for the necessary hookups for my laptop and replied, "Looks like I'm good to go. Thank you."

"Just ring me if you need anything," she said, turning to exit the boardroom. "I'll come back to escort you out when you are done."

So I began the day's executive briefing, once again the lone woman in a roomful of men.

The Only Woman in the Room
The year was 2003. Week after week that year, I crisscrossed the U.S., Canada, and Mexico, leading informative dialogs with the senior officers of Arrow's largest accounts. I typically met with the CEO, COO, VP of manufacturing, VP of engineering, chief legal counsel or compliance officer, the director of procurement, and some of their direct reports. Once the executive assistant had departed, I was typically the only woman in the room.

I was quite accustomed to a career working in male-dominated organizations. However, on the three-hour flight home that day after this particular briefing, I realized that enough was enough. I had been the only woman in this series of C-level briefings one too many times.

I relaxed in my seat and closed my eyes. One by one, I pictured the various organizations I had worked for over the years, starting with the first Fortune 100 I had gone to work for upon completion of my MBA two decades earlier. Back then, as one of the many newly minted female MBAs hired that year, the term *male-dominated* never even entered my mind.

Most everyone in my University of Rhode Island MBA class of 1982 understood the importance of having at least one mentor or sponsor to guide them up the career ladder. As one of the first employees of American Bell, the newly deregulated arm of AT&T launched in January of 1983, I set out to meet a few senior-level women in the sales organization to which I was assigned. I quickly discovered that while there were several entry-level professional women within my organization, there were very few women in mid-level management and there were none at the higher levels within our region.

I immediately set out to get acquainted with one of the few female sales directors in our building. To say her response to me was lukewarm is being kind. It took just one informational interview with her to decide I did not want to be like her. I decided to pursue mentor options elsewhere within the organization.

Interestingly, I found the male managers and directors to be much more open and willing to serve as advisors to me as I embarked on my new career journey. With plenty of bright young female peers within the sales and systems engineering entry-level ranks, I was confident we would figure out how to climb the career ladder together.

Five years later, I joined IBM, where I initially reported to a trailblazing African American woman named Melody. Within six months, Melody was promoted and relocated to take on a regional marketing director position. I was thrilled for her. To me, her promotion meant women were being groomed for bigger roles higher up, provided they were willing to relocate to wherever the available position happened to be.

I remember my first high-visibility promotion to business development manager, which gave me the unique opportunity to forge product development relationships between IBM and some of the world's largest telecommunications companies. It was a wonderful growth opportunity for me to meet with the CEOs of these potential IBM business partners on behalf of Ellen Hancock, the senior vice president of IBM's network systems division. My self-confidence and my career flourished as a result.

Although IBM did not have a female CEO during my tenure there, it was clear that several brilliant women were being groomed for IBM's top spot. I never doubted that I could get there, too, if I was willing to do the hard work.

IBM eventually did promote a woman to the top spot in 2012: Ginni Rometty. Just like me, Ginni began her IBM career as a systems engineer, followed by a move into

I never doubted that I could get there, too, if I was willing to do the hard work.

sales, and then on to a leadership role in IBM's professional services division.

I subsequently moved on to Arrow Electronics, where I reported directly to a go-getting female vice president, Cathy. She quickly became my good friend, mentor, and sponsor. Cathy supported me in taking high-visibility assignments where I not only met with the C-level executives of our largest global accounts, but I also had frequent contact with our own CEO and chairman of the board. There was no doubt in my mind that Cathy and I were both headed to the top.

My exposure to the C-suites of the high-tech industry turned out to be quite an awakening. In one executive briefing after another, I rarely met with other women. At first, I shrugged it off as an anomaly. But as time went by, I came to realize all-male C-suites were the norm, not the exception. The executive briefing on this day became the proverbial last straw.

A Mid-Flight Awakening

As I reflected on my career and the events of the day, the flight attendant offered me a beverage. I gratefully replied, "Yes, I'll have a red wine, thank you."

As I took my first sip, I wondered, *What happened to all those women in my MBA program? Why is it that so few technology companies have women in their C-suites?*

I thought back to all my client visits. I had observed plenty of women on factory floors and in supply chain procurement roles. There were plenty of women in technology sales positions. Women were even in engineering, albeit not many. Of course, human resources and marketing departments were full of women.

Why, then, were so few women moving into the top spots within these functional areas? Why were so few women found in P&L-responsible roles? Was this situation unique to the technology industry? Were women in Fortune 100 companies outside my industry running lines of business? If women were not rising to the top spots in most industries, what was holding them back?

I took another sip of wine and reviewed my own career decisions. If anything or anyone had ever held me back from moving up the ladder, it was a result of my own deliberate choices. More than once, I chose to outlive an empty-suit boss, or I chose to take a side-step around a roadblock, or I elected to stall in a holding pattern to accommodate a family priority. In no case did a lack of self-confidence or ambition ever hold me back. Quite the contrary.

If women were not rising to the top spots in most industries, what was holding them back?

That was the moment, at 30,000 feet above it all, that I realized, I had always been so focused on successfully advancing my own career—while being the perfect wife, raising brilliant children, and helping the amazing women just above and below me in my own little world get ahead—I had failed to realize there was a bigger challenge to overcome. That was the awakening that stirred the embers of my soul to become an advocate to help other women everywhere succeed in reaching the highest echelons of business.

By the end of my flight home, I vowed to start paying more attention to the composition of C-suites beyond the technology industry.

I finished my glass of wine, put up my tray table, and prepared for landing.

Navigating a Sea of Suits and Ties

Until that day in 2003, I had never paid much attention to the published statistics about the number of Fortune 500 CEOs who were women. I was stunned to discover a few days later that women held just 1.4 percent of the CEO positions in the Fortune 500 that year.

I rationalized that rising to the level of CEO in a Fortune 500 company takes time. Women with MBA degrees *and* some years of P&L experience were just now coming of age.

It was just prior to my arrival on the big business scene, in the early 1980s, that Fortune 100 companies like AT&T and IBM instituted quota-based programs to hire, develop, and promote women into management positions. Women like me, who had benefited from such programs, were just now beginning to reach the senior ranks.

The most senior women in management I knew had about 30 years of tenure. Now at the 20-year mark myself, I was quite satisfied with how far I had come and where I was headed. With my VP boss, Cathy, forging the way, it seemed certain I would follow in her footsteps to the top of the ladder at Arrow. Yet, I was well aware that very few women pursued the type of positions Cathy and I held in the technology world.

Time passed quickly, as it does. Life moved on, taking several unexpected turns along the way, and before I knew it, six years had gone by. After an opportunity to move into a C-suite position in another global technology firm failed to pan out as expected, enough was enough. I made the monumental decision to leave the relative safety of corporate America to pursue life as an entrepreneur dedicated to accelerating the advancement of women into senior leadership roles in big business.

I will explain more in the next chapter about the situation that finally caused me to take that quantum leap from corporate leadership to entrepreneurship. For now, suffice it to say that it was one man's bias regarding women's role in the workplace that drove me to forge a new path to fulfilling what ultimately became my career's most compelling mission.

My Leap into Entrepreneurship...and Women's Leadership Advocacy

When I initially ventured out on my own in 2009, I honestly had no idea how I would go about my newly defined mission. Yet, armed with the self-confidence gained from years of creating new organizations within major corporations, one after another, literally from scratch, I had no doubt I could succeed in my new mission.

At the time I made that fateful decision, I honestly had no idea if women even wanted to be at the top. Yet I assumed at least some women wanted to make it to C-suite-level positions. Thus, I set out to understand what was preventing them from getting there. I wanted to know the stumbling blocks standing in the way so I could better determine how to remove them.

Once again, I reviewed the latest statistics. By 2009, the percentage of female Fortune 500 CEOs had by now more than doubled, from 1.4 percent in 2003, to 3 percent. It was not much of a gain, but at least the momentum was headed in the right direction.

So, I assembled a start-up team. I enlisted the support of three professional women friends, each of whom had been a casualty of the 2008 financial crisis—a senior VP and corporate controller of a nationwide residential lender, a VP of information technology for a well-known toy manufacturer, and a director of operations for a big four accounting firm. Each had a wealth of knowledge, each was as passionate about this mission as I was, and each agreed to join me in creating the business plan for my start-up venture.

Over the next six months, we designed a multi-tiered leadership development program for women at each step of the management career ladder—from high-potential individual contributors to C-suite executives.

Our goal was to create a stronger pipeline of women leaders through a membership-based peer mentoring program. The participants could progress through the various tiers of our program as they were promoted through the leadership ranks to the top.

We launched Business Women Rising, Inc., in November 2009. We hired leadership trainers and executive coaches who had worked in Fortune 100 companies.

The focus for our entry-level through mid-level manager programs was to help them develop stronger strategic thinking skills and greater self-confidence. We helped our executive-level members foster greater innovation and engagement within their organizations.

Our peer mentoring sessions were strictly confidential, non-judgmental environments that allowed for frank discussion of sensitive information. Every participant was free to ask any kind of question and express their inner-most thoughts and concerns without fear of reprisal. No two members in any one group were from the same company.

Not only did every participant develop stronger leadership skills and more confidence in their own decision-making abilities, they also became more comfortable with just being themselves. They proactively pursued stretch assignments. Within their first year in the program,

Within their first year in the program, virtually every participant received at least one promotion.

virtually every participant received at least one promotion.

My team and I measured our own performance based on our members' rate of promotion. Most importantly, we came to understand—and enabled our participants to overcome—the obstacles, stumbling blocks, and circumstances that can hinder one's progression up the ladder.

By the middle of our second year in operation, I realized we needed a better way to quickly get all our participants, at every level of management, on the same page in terms of understanding my own personal leadership philosophies about the four areas of focus for our program, which were:

1. What it takes to build and lead a "Best Place to Work" organization
2. What it takes to be the kind of leader people love to follow
3. How to identify and overcome the myriad of obstacles that can get in the way
4. What it takes to position for and thrive in executive leadership

I eventually concluded that we needed a book for our participants, at every level of management, to read and absorb upon entering our program. So, I set out on a new adventure—to become an author.

I must admit, that little book project became a much bigger effort than I originally envisioned. But once I got into the research and writing process, I became increasingly passionate about the undertaking. I also realized there was a far bigger audience hungry for such information. Ultimately, what began as a plan to write one book became a four-book endeavor.

The first book, *The WOW Factor Workplace: How to Create a Best Place to Work Culture*, published in early 2020, addressed the first area of focus listed above. The second book, *Heartfelt Leadership: How to Capture the Top Spot and Keep on Soaring*, published just four months later, addressed the second area. The book you are now reading—or listening to—addresses the third focus area, and a fourth book to address the final topic is forthcoming.

A Book of Women's Voices

This book is for every woman—from any walk of life, on any career path, within any industry, and at any step on her career ladder—who aspires to executive leadership. This book is designed to help you identify and overcome the myriad of hidden roadblocks that can get in your way.

As with my first two books, *The WOW Factor Workplace* and *Heartfelt Leadership*, this book is chock-full of incredibly personal, real-life stories of down-to-earth, yet highly successful C-level executives.

What is different about this book from my first two is that it specifically highlights the real-world experiences and insights of *women* who have made it to the top in the corporate world, the not-for-profit world, the military and government, and beyond.

Within these pages, you will hear from seven inspirational women who have "been there, done that"…and who remained true to themselves in the process of reaching the top. Each one will share the ups and downs of her career along with the valuable lessons she learned along the way. You will hear how each of them overcame the odds to achieve success beyond her wildest expectations.

Each woman highlighted in this book was selected because she also met the very narrow qualifications that I required of the executives featured in my first two books. Each *woman on top* featured in the pages that follow exemplifies heartfelt leadership, and each has been recognized for the "Best Place to Work" cultures they created along the way.

Throughout this book, I will also share with you my own lessons learned during my 30 years in the trenches of corporate America, along with the eye-opening insights I gained while coaching and mentoring scores of high-potential women during my decade-plus as the CEO of a leadership development company.

The primary purpose of this book is to help you get out of your own way as you climb the leadership ladder. It is my hope that by the end of this book, you will not only have the confidence to step forward and accept high-visibility stretch opportunities, but you will also proactively *ask* for them. I also hope that you will become more aware of the value of your personal brand. And I hope that you will shine like a superstar as you gracefully navigate around any obstacle that might appear in your path.

While I am not advocating for organizations to set quotas for women in C-suite positions, I do find it encouraging that more women are moving into the C-suites of America than ever before. As of this writing, 8 percent of Fortune 500 CEOs are women. The trend toward more women on top is gaining momentum. Just imagine: You could be one of them.

The trend toward more women on top is gaining momentum. Just imagine: You could be one of them.

Now read on. May the insights and advice in the ensuing chapters lead to your own great awakening.

INTROSPECTIONS:

1 Are you serious about becoming an executive-level leader? Why or why not?

2 Does your boss consider you to be a high-potential candidate? Why or why not?

3 Do you make a habit of asking for stretch assignments? Why or why not?

4 If you have ever been offered a high-visibility assignment, did you accept it? Why or why not?

5 Do you believe women have a moral responsibility to lift up other women?

TWO

Inflection Points

Often we look so long at the closed door that we do not see the one that has been opened for us.
-HELEN KELLER

A few years after the executive briefing that I described in the opening chapter, Arrow Electronics—where I worked at that time—made some surprising and dramatic changes within its board of directors and senior leadership ranks. My VP boss and mentor, Cathy, who had done so much to give me unbridled access to the C-suite, left the company. I never saw that coming.

Given how close we were, I was surprised that she exited without at least giving me a heads-up. She obviously knew things I was not privy to. Perhaps her resignation was not her choice. She never told me, even years later.

Upon Cathy's departure, her position was eliminated. The organization I ran was merged into another, and things were never the same. I did my best to protect my team from the upheaval of the reorganization, but I slowly lost that lovin' feelin' for the business. Without a sponsor like Cathy forging the path ahead, I knew in my heart my visions of career success were not going to happen there, at least not anytime soon.

I looked around for other leadership opportunities, both inside and outside the company. With nearly ten years invested there, I did not necessarily want to leave Arrow, but I knew I needed to assess my value outside the company. Not wanting to jump from the frying pan into the fire, I took my time exploring as I continued to give my best to the role I had.

As the months passed, I weighed the merits of alternative internal offers. Each had downsides, the biggest being that none would have me reporting to the executive team at headquarters, as I always had. Each was a lateral side step. None of them seemed exciting.

Then, out of the blue, an intriguing external possibility landed in my lap with a network technology manufacturer headquartered within easy driving distance of my home. This piqued my interest.

Part of what I am about to share was discussed in my second book, *Heartfelt Leadership*. But since our focus here is on what is keeping you from executive leadership, I am now going to tell you the rest of that story—my show-stopping encounter with culture-based gender discrimination. What happened to me was so shocking, it changed the trajectory of my career.

This interesting new external opportunity was with a company I was familiar with. I had met with several of their executive team members while conducting all those executive briefings described in the previous chapter. I was quite aware it was a male-dominated company.

What happened to me was so shocking, it changed the trajectory of my career.

During my initial conversations with the recruiter, I was told that the company's co-founder, who served as the CEO and chairman, had brought a new president onboard some months before—an executive from IBM's Network Systems Division. This new president wanted to change the culture a bit by bringing a strong female leader into the senior leadership ranks. He intended to make his mark, in part, by building a more inclusive culture.

I was intrigued with the opportunity for a couple of reasons: 1) I would likely have a great deal in common with the new president, given our mutual backgrounds within IBM's Network Systems Division, and 2) given the proximity of the company's corporate headquarters to my home, I would not need to relocate for an eventual C-suite assignment.

Red Flags in the Hiring Process

I was informed that successful completion of the interview process required affirmative votes by all thirteen vice presidents, all of whom were men. I felt up to the challenge and agreed to give it a go. Upon receiving the interview schedule, however, a little red flag went up in the back of my mind. The series of four to five interviews per day, scheduled over three consecutive days, was no problem, but I was concerned that there was no interview scheduled with the president or the CEO/chairman.

When I raised my concern to the recruiter, she responded, "Not to worry. The CEO is traveling in India for the rest of the month, and the president also has a hectic travel schedule meeting clients. If you get the thumbs-up from all thirteen VPs, the president is confident the two of you will hit it off. For now, he is just anxious for you to get started without him."

I knew instinctively what she was referring to. Most of us who were hired into IBM *back in the day* were cut from the same cloth. Most every IBMer met a certain standard, in terms of work ethic and behavior. Most all managers had gone through the same leadership training.

But when I pressed her about meeting with the CEO/chairman, the recruiter brushed my question aside by saying, "The CEO/chairman is stepping away from the day-to-day operations now that the new president is onboard. Between you and me, he's grooming the president to become CEO."

I was more intrigued hearing the new president was slated to become the CEO. This likely meant that additional women would be brought onboard as well. The male-dominated culture would indeed change. I could be the one to lead the way.

The ensuing interview process went well. The recruiter called me the following week to say an

The male-dominated culture would indeed change. I could be the one to lead the way.

offer would be forthcoming from one of the VPs. But when the hiring VP called to extend the offer, he began by saying, "Now, keep an open mind." *Red flag.*

He went on to say that, at least for the immediate term, the position would start one level below what we had originally discussed. "But only for the time being," he insisted. *Red flag.*

Apparently, that was the only way they could bring me onboard without the president's signoff, while he was away. The VP assured me they were just trying to bring me onboard as quickly as possible. Things would get straightened out once the president was back in town. "Trust me," he said. *Red flag.*

I had learned long before to never accept a promise of something to be done retroactively. Never trust a compensation package or title adjustment to be made after the fact. Whatever is not negotiated up front, is not in the cards.

"I'll need time to think about it," I responded.

Whatever is not negotiated up front, is not in the cards.

Over the next two weeks, I had several more conversations with the recruiter and the hiring VP. They confided in me about a series of orchestrated moves that were supposedly in the works:

- The CEO/chairman would soon become the executive chairman. With that change, he would step away from the day-to-day operations.
- The president would then become CEO.
- The hiring VP would become president.
- I would then backfill the hiring VP's position.

It sounded plausible.

But there was still that little red flag. I kept asking myself, *Would I really want to leave Arrow without a VP title up front? What if this sequence of events does not play out?*

I evaluated and reevaluated the pros and cons of each internal and external opportunity I had in the works and continued to negotiate with the hiring VP over the external opportunity. Once they met my compensation and benefits expectations, I decided to take the risk and accepted their offer.

A Leap into the Unknown

When I notified Arrow of my planned departure, most everyone there was stunned. "You've been here almost ten years. You cannot leave. What will it take to keep you?"

As far as I was concerned, I had already given Arrow plenty of time to make it work for me. With things so upside down from all the changes in the C-suite, the executive team seemed far more concerned about themselves than anyone else. I was done. I served out my obligatory two weeks and then set out on vacation to

French Polynesia with my husband to clear my head and refresh my soul before embarking on my next career adventure.

When I arrived home from vacation on the Saturday evening before starting the new job, I found a voicemail message waiting from my soon-to-be boss: "I am sorry to call you on a weekend, but I wanted to give you a heads-up. Some surprises happened Friday. I'll fill you in when you get here on Monday."

What was that supposed to mean? Had my new boss been promoted to president already? Would I be moving into the VP position on Monday? If he had good news, wouldn't he have simply shared it then?

On Monday morning, I found my new boss waiting for me in the lobby. He informed me the new president—the former IBMer— had been fired the prior Friday afternoon. The CEO/chairman would now also be serving as acting-president. *Big red flag.*

"Do I still have a job?" I asked.

"Yes, of course. Nothing else changed."

"They didn't name you as president?"

"No."

"When do you think that will happen?"

"I don't know."

This new situation gave me grave cause for concern. I had not even met with the CEO/chairman during the interview process and now he would be my second-line manager.

My gut instinct was to rescind my acceptance of their offer. This was not at all what I had expected. There was certainly no reason to believe that the series of orchestrated moves that had been laid out to me would take place anytime soon.

Against my better judgment, I made the snap decision to stay, at least for the time being. I'd give it a chance to play out. Maybe there would still be a pony in here somewhere. There were certainly no ponies to be found back at Arrow at this point.

I'd give it a chance to play out. Maybe there would still be a pony in here somewhere.

No news came forth that week.

As the days went on, it became more and more clear that the CEO/chairman/now acting-president was going to run the business his own way. He was not about to change the culture of the company. He would not be stepping away from the day-to-day operations anytime soon.

The more I thought about it, I recalled hearing about the CEO/chairman's background. He had originally come to the United States from India as a young man, with just $10 in his pocket and without a place to stay, to obtain a master's degree in electrical engineering. He eventually became quite successful. It was an impressive story.

I rationalized that I had worked with numerous male engineers of Asian and Indian descent over the years. I never once felt any reluctance on their parts to work with me. I was quite adept at building solid relationships with virtually everyone. Certainly, once the CEO/chairman got to know me, he would come to appreciate and respect me. I would do my best to make the situation work, despite the little red flag in my head that refused to go away.

About a month into the new job, my VP boss invited me to attend an executive committee meeting so he could formally introduce me as the new head of Global Business Operations and give me his public endorsement. I looked forward to meeting the CEO.

But the CEO did not attend the meeting.

Some Disheartening Developments

Another month passed, and my boss once again invited me to attend the next executive committee meeting, this time to present my organization's operating plans. But shortly before that meeting started, my boss sent me an urgent email to let me know I had been removed from the agenda. I was not to attend.

Yet another month went by, and I still had not met the CEO. So, I asked the CEO's executive assistant to schedule a brief one-on-one for us to meet. She responded that the CEO was too busy to meet with me. There was no time available on his calendar for the foreseeable future.

Eventually, I attended a meeting where the CEO was to be present; however, he was the last person to enter the room. During the meeting, he never looked my way or acknowledged my presence. At the end of the meeting, I tried to introduce myself, but he seemed to deliberately ignore me. He spoke only to certain men in the room and then made a quick exit. I wondered if it was me.

He spoke only to certain men in the room and then made a quick exit. I wondered if it was me.

Meanwhile, my VP boss and I developed a great relationship, and I made the rounds to get to know the other department heads. I spent my time trying to understand how my organization could best help them.

My boss was delighted with the speed at which my organization made positive impacts on the business. My team took on seemingly impossible and otherwise failing projects from other departments. We not only completed those projects on time and under budget, but we also received accolades from stakeholders, both inside and outside the company.

Within no time, my boss became a great champion of mine, and I mentored him in return. Life was good even though the CEO/ chairman continued to ignore me.

About six months into the job, other vice presidents started confiding in me that they thought my boss was finally poised to take over as president. I waited anxiously for that announcement as the clock kept ticking away.

After working there nine months, I still had not met one-on-one with the CEO. I occasionally saw him around campus, but he never slowed down long enough to even acknowledge me. It was as though I were invisible. He always seemed either deep in thought or deep in conversation with one of the male executives.

One Friday afternoon, one of my staff members who had an office two doors down from my boss stepped into my office and closed the door. He whispered that he had just overheard that my boss had been called into an urgent meeting with the CEO. "Maybe he's finally getting promoted," he said. I simply raised my eyebrows and shrugged my shoulders.

I waited around until almost everyone else had gone home, hoping to catch my boss return to his office after his meeting with the CEO, but he never came back. At 7:00 p.m., concerned that there might have been a serious problem, I walked out to the parking lot. My boss's car was gone, so I went home.

Upon arrival on Monday morning, I headed straight to my boss's office, only to find it emptied of all his personal belongings. When his executive assistant arrived, she came straight to my office to tell me the news. Our boss had been fired.

An announcement came out later that morning under the CEO's signature. It said our VP had resigned to pursue other interests. I knew better than that. Only then did it dawn on me: I now reported directly to the CEO. He did not know me at all.

> **Only then did it dawn on me: I now reported directly to the CEO. He did not know me at all.**

My now-more-urgent attempts to schedule a one-on-one with him continued to fail. The only answers I would hear from his executive assistant were, "I'm sorry. He's completely booked," or, "He's out of town for the foreseeable future."

Eventually, a new senior VP of sales was brought onboard, and my organization was merged under him. Given the operational nature of my organization, this reorganization did not seem to make much sense, but it was not my decision to make. Nevertheless, I focused on building a relationship with him. At least there was now someone between me and the CEO. I never would have thought I would be better off *not* reporting directly to a CEO.

The new SVP seemed pleasant enough, although he did not seem terribly interested in learning much about my organization or the tremendous benefits we were delivering to the company. He simply kept asking me, "Why are you working on that?" or, "Who came up with that idea?"

A Crushing Blow

About a month after the SVP's arrival, his assistant called me one morning and asked me to come to his office. When I arrived, I found him seated at his desk, staring into oblivion. He would not look at me. As I sat down in the chair opposite him, I noticed the VP of human resources standing in the corner. *Red flag.*

This is it, I thought to myself. I took a deep breath and looked straight at my SVP boss.

He continued to look away in silence. I noticed his eyes watering. Finally, I said, "You want to tell me what's going on?"

He continued to sit in silence and then suddenly stood up, saying, "I can't do this," as he walked out of the office.

With that, I turned to the VP of HR and raised my eyebrows. He flatly said, "You're being released. The head of security is just outside the door to escort you to your desk. You will find boxes on your desk for your belongings. You have fifteen minutes to be off the premises. You can hand me your ID badge now."

As the VP of HR exited, the head of security came in to escort me to my office. I knew him well. We chatted each morning when I entered the building.

As we walked together back to my office, he told me how sorry he was. I told him this was a first for me. I had never been laid off or fired before.

This was a first for me. I had never been laid off or fired before.

"You're not the only one," he said as he shook his head.

When we reached my department, I found all but one of the female managers I had hired onto my team packing up their own belongings. As I walked past the first one—a very professional black woman I had hired just a few months before—I asked incredulously, "Have you been laid off?"

With a bitter tone in her voice she responded, "You mean you don't know?"

"No. I had no idea. I've been laid off, too."

"You're kidding me. They're laying *you* off?"

I then noticed all the men on my department were working, heads down, trying to ignore what was going on. Once inside my office, as I picked up a box to start packing, one of my guys stepped in and stated in disbelief, "Oh my God, did you get laid off, too?"

"Yes."

"Oh, no! What are we going to do?"

With that, the head of security warned me there was no time for conversation. He offered to help me pack and then walked me out of the building. That was that.

When I arrived home, a voice mail message was waiting from my former VP boss—the one who had been fired several weeks before. Apparently, someone from my team had called him at home to share what had happened that morning. His voice mail message said, "I'm so sorry this has happened to you. You didn't do anything wrong. This is not about you."

But it was about me. This happened to *me*. I could not help but feel disappointed in

I had plenty of chances to walk out on my own terms, but I didn't. I foolishly played the Pollyanna.

myself. I had ignored so many red flags. I should have known better. I had plenty of chances to walk out on my own terms, but I didn't. I foolishly played the Pollyanna.

Over the next few days, several former peers and professional friends called to check in and coach me. Most urged me not to sign the severance papers. They confirmed that all but the most junior woman on my staff had been laid off that same day, yet none of the men in my department were let go. Apparently, a few men were laid off in other departments as the result of a "corporate downsizing," but then, most of the company was comprised of men.

One of my staff members faxed me a report distributed by the human resources department that provided the details of the layoff. The report "proved" the layoff was equally balanced by gender, race, and age group. I could not help but wonder if those men in the other departments were laid off to make it appear that the downsizing was not discriminatory.

Several friends urged me to hire an attorney to fight what appeared to them to be wrongful termination. They encouraged me to file a gender discrimination lawsuit. I quickly decided

I simply did not want to spend the next several months haggling over a lawsuit. I just wanted to get on with my career.

against doing so. I simply did not want to spend the next several months haggling over a lawsuit. I just wanted to get on with my career.

I eventually came to learn that virtually everyone involved in my hiring—my VP boss, the president from IBM, and even the recruiter—had all been let go. Every female manager I had brought onboard was let go. It seemed clear to me that the CEO/chairman did not want women in leadership positions, nor did he want anyone else working for him who had the audacity to hire a woman into a management capacity.

One year later, the SVP who could not bring himself to lay me off left the company. Within five years, the CEO/chairman died of cardiac arrest and the company was sold.

My Ultimate Inflection Point

In the words of Andy Grove, former CEO of Intel Corporation, "A strategic inflection point is a time…when fundamentals are about to change. That change can mean an opportunity to rise to new heights. But it may just as likely signal the beginning of the end."

Looking back, I now know the moment that I was let go was the ultimate inflection point of my career. I had come to the end of my climb within corporate America, yet I was not done rising to new heights.

As I walked out of that corporate headquarters for the last time, carrying my boxes of personal effects, I became more determined than ever to do whatever was within my power to ensure such things would not happen to other women. It was time for me to move full steam ahead to accelerate advancement for women to executive leadership. I just had to figure out how.

REFLECTIONS:

There were so many should haves/would haves/could haves.

- I knew from the outset to never accept an offer with a contingency attached. I should have terminated the negotiations the first time the hiring VP told me to "keep an open mind" and then failed to deliver the full offer package I expected.
- On the day I first arrived, when I learned the president had been fired, I should have rescinded my acceptance of their offer.
- Once it became obvious to me that I was invisible to the CEO/chairman—when he never acknowledged me, when it was clear he had no intention of ever meeting with me—I should have faced the fact that I would likely never be able to change his mind.
- I should have realized I was never going to be promoted to VP while he was still in the business.
- At each of these inflection points, I should have put on a full-court press to find a more suitable position elsewhere.

In hindsight, I do not believe the CEO/chairman was biased from a racial perspective. The company was full of men of all different races and ethnicities.

I do not believe the CEO/chairman was biased against women in general. His executive assistant was a woman, as were all the administrative assistants I knew in the company.

I do not believe the CEO/chairman was biased against me specifically. He did not even know me and he clearly had no intent to ever get to know me.

But based on what I saw happen, it seemed to me that he was biased against women serving in leadership roles within his own company.

In the end, I never did figure out what, if anything, I had personally done to precipitate my termination—other than being an overly optimistic, self-confident woman who was in the wrong place at the wrong time. But whatever the real reason was, I learned the hard way that being let go is not fun.

Admittedly, my termination was not a surprise. There had been so many warning signs along the way. I just chose to ignore the many signs, sometimes against my better judgment. I never stopped assuming I could overcome any and every obstacle in my path, just as I had done throughout my entire career.

But, regardless of one's own self-confidence or dogged determination, none of us are infallible. There are always others who hold more sway or more power, whether it's the CEO, or the board of directors, a vengeful peer, an upset client, or the press. We must acknowledge the road signs as they present themselves and change tack accordingly, especially if we're heading toward Niagara Falls.

Yet, in the words of the late Robert F. Kennedy, "Only those who dare to fail greatly can ever achieve greatly."

I am an admitted overachiever. Always have been. Always will be. I now invite you to join me on the journey to achieving greatly.

INTROSPECTIONS:

1 Have you ever accepted a job offer that was less than you expected and believed you deserved? If so, why did you accept it?

2 Have you ever reported to an up-line manager who was raised in a culture that believes a woman's place is not in leadership? If so, how did that up-line manager treat you? Did it offend you?

3 Have you ever remained in a position with no apparent possibility of promotion? If so, why did you stay and what were the results?

4 What would you have done had you been in my shoes in the situation described above?

THREE

Higher Education

If obtaining a particular degree is indeed a requirement, or even if it is simply something you would like to do and you can afford the investment, then go for it. But never let higher education, or the lack thereof, keep you from executive leadership.

-DEB BOELKES

fter I left corporate America in 2009 and established my leadership development company, Business Women Rising, of the myriad of issues we discovered that can hold women back from executive leadership, having the "right" college or advanced degree was one of the most surprising, at least to me. I became acutely aware of this stumbling block the more I addressed audiences of women attending various undergraduate, graduate, and post-graduate programs. I presented one such example in Chapter Seven of my book *The WOW Factor Workplace: How to Create a Best Place to Work Culture*. For this reason, I'm addressing this topic right up front.

While it has not always been the norm, for the past several decades, high school guidance counselors have encouraged students to attend college, be it a trade school, a two-year community college, or a four-year university and beyond. In general, college graduates have more earning potential over a lifetime than those with only a high school diploma.

Some young people discover early in life that they have a calling—to be a doctor, a lawyer, a musician, or whatever. But most of us are not lucky enough to have a calling, so we take the ride to discover the kinds of things that stir our passions. Either way, college can be an eye-opening bridge between childhood and adulthood. It can be a great way to become more self-aware, test your abilities, come out of your shell, and discover what really turns you on—or not.

On the other hand, major universities have become absurdly overpriced when you perform the cost/benefit assessment. Not only does a four-year degree from a big-name school come with a huge price tag, spending four or more years of one's life in college is a big investment of time. College can be a complete waste of time if the student is not learning to think critically or is drifting aimlessly, without a career objective.

Based on my own experience obtaining an associate in arts degree, a bachelor of science degree, and an MBA, along with my experience as a parent who sent two sons through college, I have concluded that students are far more apt to make wiser decisions about investing in higher education if they have a significant personal stake in paying for it.

Whether or not you attend college, it is important to discover who you are and then

> **I have concluded that students are far more apt to make wiser decisions about investing in higher education if they have a significant personal stake in paying for it.**

be true to yourself. Finding who you are—and learning to become a self-reliant, successful adult—can happen at college, or through experience in the military, by traveling the world, through volunteering, or by working in various trades. There is no one right answer.

Some of us gain a fabulous education and come to discover who we were always meant to be by trying all of the above, over time.

My College Journey Begins

None of my grandparents had much education beyond the eighth grade. Both of my parents attended college, and they wanted the same for me. It was simply assumed I would attend a major university upon graduating high school.

Despite being an overachiever throughout my early years, I did virtually no research when it came time to apply to college. Most of my high school friends simply went to one of three major universities in our state. It is almost laughable now, but back in the mid-1970s, the standard assumption in my high school was this:

- Those who were smart but had limited funds went to the University of California, Los Angeles (UCLA).
- Those who had plenty of money but mediocre grades went to the University of Southern California (USC).
- Those who were very smart, and for whom money was no object, went to Stanford.

Therefore, I applied to only one school and attended UCLA, where I thought I belonged.

When my biological mother passed away, my father had significant medical expenses to pay. As a result, he told me he would be able to pay for my room and board and school tuition for only the first two years, provided I took a full course load and kept my grades up. Spending money and the cost of everything else would be up to me. At the end of those two years, I would be completely responsible for myself, financially and otherwise. That was quite an incentive to buckle down and grow up.

Without even reviewing the hundreds of options for majors in the UCLA catalog, I simply picked a double major: math/computer science, primarily because math was my strong suit. I figured it would be an easy major. Besides, I already had a year of college credit for calculus, thanks to scoring well on the advanced placement (AP) math exams in high school. By immediately jumping into second-year calculus, I figured I could get through college even faster.

I honestly had no idea what computer science was, but my father had always said that computers were the way of the future. That was the extent of my thought process in terms of selecting a major.

So, at age 17, off I went to UCLA, with all the self-confidence in the world. I went through rush and joined the Chi Omega sorority, primarily because the cost of living in a sorority, at that time, was less than living in a dormitory. Thankfully, the sorority gave me the love, direction, and sisterly mentorship I did not even know I needed.

My first day of class was a real eye-opener. As I walked into my Physics 101 class, I was stunned to find myself *not* in a 30-person classroom—the kind we had in high school—but in a huge, 650-seat theater. As I stood at the rear entrance of the lecture theater, it appeared as though every seat was already taken. I could barely even see the professor, way down below at the front of the hall.

As I scanned the rows and rows of seats, desperately trying to find an empty spot where I could sit, I did not see any other woman in the class. For the first time since I arrived on campus, I was scared.

Later that week, I attended my first physics lab. I breathed a sigh of relief to find the lab almost cozy by comparison. Led by a young teaching assistant (TA) rather than a professor, there were just 40 students in the lab. Even though I was (again) the only woman in the room, I felt a bit more comfortable here.

About halfway into the lab session, the TA instructed us to form small cohorts of three or four students, as lab study teams. Not one guy in the class invited me to join his study team, so I found a group that had only three guys and introduced myself. Their lack of enthusiasm surprised me. I only wanted to join a team…but I realized at that moment I did not fit in.

> **I only wanted to join a team…but I realized at that moment I did not fit in.**

I barely survived that year. While I enjoyed living in the sorority, and I had fun attending football and basketball games, I did not enjoy my classes. Worst of all, I could not figure out what I would do with a math/computer science degree. Certainly, none of my sorority sisters had any clue. Not one of the 90 women in the Chi O house majored in math or computer science, let alone both. Midway through the year, I concluded this double major was not for me.

I had to do some soul searching about the kinds of things I really loved to do. Although I was good at math, I did not enjoy the classes. Nor did I love my computer science classes, which required me to spend hours in the computer lab, keypunching those silly rectangular cards. I found that tedious and boring. It seemed clear that I had landed in the wrong place.

A Sudden Change of Direction
Almost on a whim, I decided to become a fashion designer.

I rationalized that since my mother had taught me to make my own clothes at an early age, and since I was quite adept at customizing most everything I made for myself, from prom dresses to party costumes, I could probably earn a good living designing women's clothing. Besides, my mother would have wanted me to head in this direction.

One of my sorority sisters, a senior, warned me that design was an impacted major at UCLA, which meant I would have to go on a two-year waiting list to get into the program. I could not afford to just hang around.

My insightful sorority sister then suggested I should apply to the Fashion Institute of Design & Merchandising (FIDM) in downtown Los Angeles. There, I could obtain an associate in arts degree in fashion design and become gainfully employed in just two years.

The downsides were that I already had one year invested at UCLA, and the tuition at FIDM was significantly more expensive than at UCLA. I needed to find some way to make it work within the limited budget and timeframe I had been granted by my father.

Upon meeting with the admissions advisor at FIDM, I discovered I could get full credit for all my UCLA classes in lieu of taking the slew of general education courses they required. I could obtain an AA degree in just twelve months if I attended through the summer, which meant I could graduate and get a good-paying job as a fashion designer within the two-year timeframe my father had stipulated.

I jumped into FIDM full steam ahead, put my nose to the grindstone, graduated with an AA degree twelve months later as the top student in the program, and immediately went to work as a fashion designer.

I spent the next five years working as a fashion designer and loved every minute of that profession. However, after observing how the owners managed the business, I concluded I would rather run my own company my way.

At that point, I decided to return to school full-time to complete my undergraduate degree, this time to obtain a bachelor's degree in business administration, to build a better foundation upon which to run a successful company. It just so happened that my husband was being reassigned to a position in Newport, Rhode Island, so it seemed like the perfect time to make the transition to business school. I applied to the University of Rhode Island, an affordable public university. To cover the costs, I took out a student loan from the bank.

When I subsequently decided to also get an MBA—with an emphasis in management information systems—I was fortunate to receive a full scholarship from the business school.

How Did My College Experience Compare to Other Women's?

As with my previous two books, when I started writing this one, I was eager to learn whether my own educational experiences and philosophies about leadership were like those of other women leading "Best Place to Work" organizations.

Before I go on, however, I must note that some of the most successful and contented people I know did not attend college. It is entirely possible to lead a major corporation without having a college degree, as did Jack Welch, former CEO of General Electric; Sam Walton, founder of Walmart; and Steve Jobs, co-founder and former CEO of Apple. Let's not forget Rachael Ray, award-winning television food star, businesswoman, and author—who not only skipped getting a bachelor's degree, she also has no formal training in the culinary arts!

Still, I was especially interested to learn whether women who had made it to the top of well-respected organizations were highly degreed, and whether they had a calling to be the one in charge, or if they simply took the ride and figured it out as they went along.

Here are a few excerpts from my conversations with powerful women on their approach to, and insights on, the world of higher education.

Melissa Reiff
Former Chairwoman and CEO
The Container Store

One of the "Best Place to Work" organizations I had wanted to highlight in my previous books was The Container Store, the only leading specialty retail chain in the United States devoted to storage and organization. Their purpose is to help their customers accomplish their projects and make the most of their home and space. Back at that time, we were unable to coordinate schedules, so one of the first executives I reached out to as I prepared to write this book was Melissa Reiff, The Container Store's then-chairwoman and CEO. I was thrilled when Melissa immediately responded with a resounding *yes*.

The Container Store first opened its doors in 1978 in a small retail space in Dallas, Texas. Since then, the company has grown dramatically, now with ninety-four stores, a growing online business, and revenues close to $1 billion. What is also impressive is the fact that this company made *Fortune* magazine's list of "100 Best Companies to Work For" for nineteen consecutive years.

Melissa, who retired from the company in March 2021 after twenty-five years, had served in numerous key leadership roles, rising to president in 2006, president and chief operating officer in 2013, and then to chief executive officer in 2016. She has served on the company's board of directors since 2007 and has served as chairwoman since August 2019, a role that she continued through August of 2021.

Melissa also serves on two other public boards: Etsy, Inc. (NASDAQ: ETSY), and Cricut Inc. (NASDAQ: CRCT). She also serves on the executive board of her alma mater, Southern Methodist University's Cox School of Business. She is a member of the International Women's Forum and C200, which are invitation-only, women-led organizations dedicated to advancing women's leadership in business.

Throughout her career, Melissa focused on enhancing and strengthening The Container Store's unique, people-first culture, which is centered on its values-based Foundation Principles. The seventh Foundation Principle—Communication IS Leadership—is a discipline that Melissa herself brought to the company.

I began our interview by asking Melissa about her educational experiences. When I asked her if she had this calling to be the CEO of a company, her answer was this:

> No. I wanted to be a lawyer. I graduated from SMU with a political science degree. Law school was going to be my path. I loved learning about the law and thought being an attorney would be challenging and interesting. However, when I was a sophomore in college, I worked with Lamar Hunt's World Championship Tennis. The tournament was held at Moody Coliseum at SMU, and I worked as a courtmate, helping to run the tournament. It was great fun and gave me the opportunity to meet lots of interesting and wonderful people.

Upon graduation, like so many young people do, I got sidetracked from my path to law school. A mentor of mine said to me at the time, "Hey, I've got an opportunity for you. I think you can do this!"

I was immediately super intrigued in exploring this opportunity. Since I had the support of my parents—which was very important to me—I took it!

Ultimately, my political science degree was put to great use and was very helpful in my retail career, because as president, COO, and CEO—some of the roles that I held at The Container Store—I worked very closely with our human resources organization and our lawyers. It all worked out beautifully, and I just fell in love with retail.

Jodi Berg
President and CEO
Vita-Mix Corporation

Jodi Berg, PhD, is the president and chief executive officer of Vita-Mix Corporation (Vitamix), a company founded by her great-grandfather a century ago.

As the fourth-generation leader of a family-owned, mid-market manufacturer of high-performance blending equipment for the consumer and foodservice commercial markets, Jodi led the company's overseas expansion into 140 countries.

Jodi is a high-energy believer that every day we have on this planet is a gift. It is up to each one of us to decide how we will make the time that we have matter. For Jodi, this means helping others discover their purpose and lead their own best lives.

When I had the pleasure of interviewing Jodi, I asked her, "Did you always work in the family business or did you prepare for working in the family business by going to college?"

> I worked in the family business when I was in high school, but I decided to do my own thing. So, I did.
>
> I got a degree in hospitality management because I realized I experienced joy in creating memorable moments and joy for others. I got a job doing just that—and I loved it!
>
> To understand the business model around memory-making, and turn the job I liked into a career, I got my MBA in service management and marketing at Washington State. While I was there, I took *one* class on quality. I absolutely fell in love with this concept of, "If it's a problem, solve it at the root so that problem doesn't exist anymore." That one class on quality changed my perspective, and I eventually combined hospitality and quality at the Ritz-Carlton Hotel Company.

I absolutely fell in love with this concept of, "If it's a problem, solve it at the root so that problem doesn't exist anymore."

> It was much later, once I was well entrenched in running the family business, that I went back to get my PhD. Very few people seek a PhD to help them with their career. I was no exception. I personally wanted to understand the science

behind the personal fulfillment and focus I got from living with purpose so maybe I could bless others with this same understanding. As it turns out, living with personal purpose will not only increase your engagement with the work you do, but it also leads to a high degree of satisfaction with life.

So, for me, higher education—although it did help with my career advancement early on—in the long run, it allowed me to succeed *and* live my life with a purpose that was personally fulfilling.

Nancy Howell Agee
President and CEO
Carilion Clinic

Nancy Howell Agee is the president and CEO of Carilion Clinic, a $2.4 billion not-for-profit integrated healthcare organization that serves nearly one million Virginians and West Virginians. Based in Roanoke, and formerly known as Carilion Health System, Carilion Clinic is comprised of a network of primary and specialty physician practices, seven hospitals, and a variety of complementary services including pharmacies and free-standing surgical clinics.

Before becoming president and CEO in 2011, Nancy served as executive vice president and chief operating officer and co-led Carilion's reorganization from a collection of hospitals to a fully integrated care delivery system.

She is a nationally recognized healthcare leader and past chair of the American Hospital Association. *Modern Healthcare* named her one of 2021's Women Leaders Luminaries that recognizes executives whose careers have been defined by reshaping the industry. She was first named to *Modern Healthcare's* biennial list of Top 25 Women Leaders in 2017 and is perennially among its 100 Most Influential People in Healthcare.

She is a member of *The Wall Street Journal* CEO Council, Virginia Foundation for Independent Colleges, Virginia Business Council, Virginia Business Higher Education Council, and the Governor's Advisory Council on Revenue Estimates. She is a fellow in the National Association of Corporate Directors.

With this impressive background, I could not wait to hear about Nancy's educational background and her early career aspirations. She had this to say about it:

> I was interested in nursing from the time I was about five years old. For Christmas I got a little nurse's outfit. Once, I was hospitalized for a long time. I had such wonderful care from very caring people that my interest was stimulated. I wanted to do something like they were doing.

> My grandmother was a real cheerleader for me. She was

My grandmother was a real cheerleader for me. She was adamant that I would go to school...She laid that pathway for me.

> adamant that I would go to school. Right from the beginning—from the time that I was in eighth grade—it was always, "When you go to college..." She laid that pathway for me.

So, I have a bachelor's degree in nursing and master's degree in nursing, also. I began my career as a nurse. I guess you could say I had that calling.

Linda Rutherford
Senior Vice President, Chief Communications Officer
Southwest Airlines

If you read either of my previous books, you know that I had the honor of interviewing some of the most amazing female members of the Southwest Airlines C-suite. Each of these women were as delightfully charming as they were inspiring.

Of all U.S. airlines, I focused on learning about Southwest's senior leadership team for several reasons. Not only has Southwest carried the most domestic passengers of any U.S. airline in the six years since 2014, but Southwest was also rated by J.D. Power as the USA's best airline for 2017 and 2018. In 2019, they tied with JetBlue for first place in overall satisfaction.

When I interviewed Southwest's chief communications officer, Linda Rutherford, I asked her to share a bit about how her early aspirations and college prepared her for her career.

I was raised by my single mom who taught me, "If you want something, you're going to have to work hard to get it."

My college degree was in journalism. While I was in college, I was actually hired as a stringer for *Newsweek* magazine. When I graduated, they offered me a job in the New York reporting bureau.

I was raised by my single mom who taught me, "If you want something, you're going to have to work hard to get it."

I was at Texas Tech University in Lubbock, Texas, at that point. I was like, "Hell, yeah! I'm going to New York!"

So, off I went. I was going to be one of those "patches on the sleeves" journalists. And I was for a while…but life had other plans for me!

While I don't have a master's degree, over the years that I have been here at Southwest, I feel like I got an MBA by just digging in and trying to learn the business the best that I could.

In Chapter Five, you'll learn a little more about Linda's transition from journalism into public relations. While the professions may look similar to an outside observer, they are very different animals. Both are built on a scaffolding of words, ideas, and communication know-how—but moving from one to the other requires quite a mind shift. So, while Linda was able to bring a lot of what she learned in college to her career, she still had to embark on a challenging journey to do what she does at Southwest Airlines.

Kerry Healey
Inaugural President
Milken Center for Advancing the American Dream

Kerry Healey, PhD, has a biography that spans a variety of impressive career paths, from being elected to serve as a state lieutenant governor, to becoming a television producer and on to becoming a university president and more. I was especially interested in interviewing her to learn how one, albeit very amazing, person could do all she has done in just one lifetime.

Today, Kerry is the inaugural president for the Milken Center for Advancing the American Dream in Washington, D.C. The Center was founded in 2019 by philanthropist Michael Milken on the belief that anyone with a dream—and the drive to achieve it—should have the opportunity to make it come true through a good education, good health, and access to the economic resources needed to succeed. Kerry is building a visitor center on the corner of Pennsylvania Avenue, across from the White House and the U.S. Treasury, that is scheduled to open on July 4, 2023, but the Center's online presence is already being felt.

During our interview, Kerry shared this about how her educational background prepared her for her very diverse leadership career.

I attended a public high school in Florida. It was severely underfunded, overcrowded, and run down. They had very few counselors, so when the time came for me to apply to college, I was greatly on my own. I had heard about Harvard, but I did not know anyone who had gone there. So, I went to the local public library, looked up where it was, wrote away for an application, and eventually got in.

I asked, "Was that the only school you applied to?"

I also applied to Duke, which is where my father had gone briefly, before going into the military in World War II. And I applied to Florida State, which is where my mother went. I had heard of Harvard, and I knew where my parents went to college. Those three were the only schools I knew about, so I applied to them all.

When I got accepted to Harvard, we were confronted with the situation that the annual tuition and the cost of housing were higher than my mother's salary. Mind you, we had lost all our money during my father's illness, a couple of years earlier. So, that was the moment when the rubber really had to hit the road.

My personal values came from my mother's strength of character. At that moment, she committed, "I believe in this notion that education is the path to success in America. I am going to give you the best education you can get. We will just figure it out. You just say *yes*. You go and we will figure it out. You will work, and I will work. We will not spend any money. We will ask our relatives for money. We'll sell whatever we've got, but you will go to college."

I then asked Kerry, "What did you major in at Harvard?"

Government. My PhD is in law and political science, so I didn't stray too far.

"Did you get a master's degree somewhere along the way?"

No. In Ireland, where I got my PhD, you do not get a master's.

Wendy Johnson
Former President and CEO
Dale Carnegie franchise, Atlanta, GA

With a diverse career, starting as an international flight attendant to leading big-ticket business-to-business sales and beyond, Wendy Johnson retired from two decades as the president and CEO of the Dale Carnegie franchise in Atlanta, Georgia. I was thrilled to meet her shortly afterward. I was most intrigued to hear Wendy's perspectives, thanks in part to the renowned reputation of the Dale Carnegie brand, known by many as the flagship provider of leadership and public communications training.

For anyone not familiar with them, Dale Carnegie has, for over a century, focused on improving individual and business performance around the world through in-person and live online courses, ranging from leadership to public speaking training. Dale Carnegie's core principles revolve around a single vision: Real transformation begins within. Dale Carnegie training is provided in over 90 countries through regional franchisees.

Wendy shared this about her educational background and early career aspirations:

> I went to the University of California at the Davis campus. I was a language major because I loved foreign languages.

I asked Wendy, "What languages did you major in?"

> Spanish and Italian.
>
> My mother was a travel agent. I would drive her to the airport whenever she was taking a familiarization trip. That is how I became enamored with the idea of travel—through the wonderful stories from her travels around the world.
>
> I realized, in my third year of college, a degree in language meant I could probably become a teacher. But I really did not want to be a teacher. I wanted to travel. So, I left college after my third year. I did not complete my college education.
>
> A defining moment was when my father passed away, during my second year of college. It was a traumatic experience, and I had to begin really supporting myself in a lot of ways. Sometimes life happens and you end up skipping some important growing up experiences. You must take on more responsibility than your years deserve.
>
> Meanwhile, the Vietnam War was raging in Cambodia. The UC Davis students were marching on campus instead of attending classes. But I was paying for my own education.

The regents of the University of California solved the problem of all the class disruption by giving every student a passing grade–after I had worked so hard the whole quarter and attended all my classes. I simply lost my initiative because of all this.

I happened to attend a presentation by a Pan Am stewardess who had been invited to campus to give a speech. I found out that Pan Am required a foreign language. That was my major, so I was gone. I was off to Pan Am and that was it.

I completed three years in good standing at UC Davis. I only had a year left, but I never finished it.

I went back to school later, a couple of times. But to graduate with something meaningful, though, I would have had to invest two more years because I would have had to change what I was majoring in.

If I had it do over again, I probably would have gotten my degree.

I asked Wendy, "Looking back, what might you have majored in to complete your degree?"

Based on what I know now, I think business would have been my major.

The funny thing about having a degree, back then, was that it did not matter what your degree was in. It was just a ticket to get a job interview. You could not get a job interview without a degree. My education really began with my six years of

traveling the
world with
Pan Am.
While I did
not get my

My education really began with my six years of traveling the world with Pan Am. While I did not get my degree, those six years were instrumental in forming a foundation for my career.

degree, those six years were instrumental in forming a foundation for my career.

I found that in the world of corporate sales, they were more lax about the requirement of having a degree because they were really looking for a particular type of person, someone with innate communication skills, which I had.

Lieutenant General Kathleen M. Gainey
U.S. Army, Retired

It was a tremendous honor to interview Lt. Gen. Kathleen M. Gainey, U.S. Army, retired. I was amazed to discover just how down-to-earth, authentic, and open she was about sharing the ups and downs of her thirty-five-plus-year military career.

While serving in the senior officer ranks, General Gainey spent twenty years leading global supply chain teams, which culminated in her assignment as deputy commander of United States Transportation Command (USTRANSCOM). Following her retirement from the military, she served as senior vice president of logistics for Cypress International, a consulting firm for companies that do business with the Department of Defense.

My discussion with General Gainey about her early career aspirations, her college experiences, and why she chose to make a lifelong commitment to the U.S. military was quite enlightening.

I really had not planned on making the military a career. I intended to be a special education teacher.

I went into the Reserve Officer Training Corps (ROTC) in college, simply because I wanted to have some extra spending money so I would not have to have as many part-time jobs while I was getting my bachelor's degree in special ed.

It made sense to me at the time. I knew that teachers got paid to work during the school year, but not in the summer. So, I figured I could be a reservist during the summers and get better pay than if I just worked at a JCPenney's or someplace else in the summer after graduation.

Besides, I kind of knew the military lingo, having been a military brat. So, I thought, *Well, that is some way I can give back to my nation, in my own way. I'll just be a reservist when I'm not teaching.*

So, I applied for that ROTC scholarship during my senior year of high school. When I got it, I said to myself, *I'll just do my three years and then get out.*

So, I went the ROTC route in college, but I could not even run a mile when I joined ROTC. I had to get physically stronger and mentally stronger. I had to learn how to adapt.

"Were you in ROTC during those first few years that women were allowed to be in ROTC?"

Yes. ROTC had just opened to women two years before I came in as a sophomore.

"Were there times while you were in college, going through ROTC, that you thought, *I am not sure this is for me*, or were you dedicated enough that you knew, *I really want to do this and I'm going to stick it out?*"

I wasn't sure. I didn't think I was going to stick it out for the long haul, but I thought, *I need a job. I am doing okay at this. I will at least come in for three years. There is nothing wrong with this. I kind of know the life I'm going to go into*, having been a military brat.

I wasn't scared of it. It was not really something I wanted to do, but it did offer something that I needed: a job. So, therefore, I thought, *If this is the only job available, then okay.*

It was not really something I wanted to do, but it did offer something that I needed: a job.

"Were you the only woman in your ROTC unit?"

No. There were five of us. They were all great gals and we helped each other.

"Five out of how many?"

One hundred ten.

"Wow. Did you all come from military families?"

No. There was just one other gal who did. Her dad had been in the Navy for twenty years. They lived right around the corner from me. So, she, Mary Maniscalco, and I became very close. We ended up carpooling together to save money.

But no one else came from a military background. We all just needed the extra money. Back then, ROTC paid $100 a month. That paid room and board for a lot of us.

"And then what happened?"

I think I gained confidence in myself, in my ability to manage, in my ability to organize, and take care of people.

"Did you start making that transition while you were in ROTC?"

Yes, the very basics.

I was a very shy person back then. When my high school friends saw that I was thinking of possibly staying in the military, when we would see each other periodically, they were like, "The body snatchers got you! This is not the Kathy Gainey we knew. The shy girl who would never even raise her hand, who would never talk...you are two different people! You are boisterous now! You are talking. You are competent. You are assertive! What happened to the Kathy Gainey we knew?"

I ultimately chose to go the active-duty route when I could
see that the special education teaching market was flooded.
The schoolteachers in special education were not getting jobs
because there had been, suddenly, such a big emphasis on
that as a career.

All the five teachers colleges in the area had graduated so
many special ed teachers in such a short period of time, there
just were not enough job opportunities to go around. So, I
thought, *Okay. I'll just go into the military.*

"Did you find a commonality with those who came from military
families? Were they the ones who stayed in and rose up the officer
ladder?"

Certainly, there were those people who, like me, kind of felt
familiar with the military and therefore gravitated to it. Maybe
some had a parent who had served at least some time in the
military. They were told, "This would be a good thing for you
to do, at least for a little bit."

Most of my friends were just like me. None of us set out to
pursue the military as a career. Mary was doing it so that she
could become a doctor. She knew that the only way she was
going to get that done was either through a full scholarship to
medical school or through the military paying for her medical
school. So, that's exactly what she did. The military paid for
her medical school. It was a means to an end for many of us.

In the military, virtually none of my friends were military brats.

"What caused you to decide to get your MBA?"

Once it was clear that I was going to have to obtain a master's degree if I wanted to advance in rank, I started pursuing it.

"Was there a certain point in your military career when a master's degree became a requirement, and did the focus of your master's degree matter?"

When you get to a certain level as an officer, about twelve years into your career, they expect you to have a master's degree. For the career-enhancing jobs, they want your master's degree to be in a field the military needs competency in.

I knew that my weakness was in financial management. Math is not my strong suit. I picked my undergrad major, special education, because it did not require any math.

But knowing that, I went to the military and asked, "What are the opportunities for graduate school?"

They came back and said, "You can get an MBA with an emphasis in either comptroller or procurement."

So, I thought, *Well, those are areas I'm weak in and either might help me enhance my career—to shore up a weakness.* So, I said okay.

I had only about one hour to decide which way to go, so I chose acquisition management (procurement), silly me. I thought there would be less math in that program. I knew it was going to be painful, but I went ahead and tried.

I tested very poorly on my graduate record examinations (GREs). I did okay in English, but terrible in the math. Babson College said, "We typically would not take anyone with scores this low," because my GMAT and GRE both were very low, even though I had taken a Kaplan course while I was stationed in Hawaii to try and prepare myself for the exams.

But then Babson said, "Look. If the military is willing to pay for you to go, we'll take you."

I just knew I was going to have to work harder. I was going to have to buckle down and learn as much as I could. That is where going to your peers, to help you learn and to mentor you, can help.

So, I would read the chapter, go to the class, listen to the lecture, write down

I just knew I was going to have to work harder. I was going to have to buckle down and learn as much as I could.

my questions, go sit with the professor, and say, "Here's what I didn't understand."

Then I would go back and reread the chapter with his clarifications.

"Did the military point you to Babson College, or did you pick where you wanted to go to school?"

When I decided to go the procurement route for my MBA, the military said, "Here are the four colleges that we typically send people to for procurement."

I had to put in applications for all four colleges that were
earmarked for procurement. If more than one accepts you,
then you can pick the college you want to go to. The military
also must approve that college. If they do, then they will fund
it.

"Then do they allow you to attend school full-time for two years,
as though it is your full-time job?"

Yes. That becomes your full-time job.

REFLECTIONS:

As our diverse sampling of women on top have illustrated, for
anyone who does not grow up with a calling—a passionate desire
to focus solely on a particular profession—college can help you
find your direction.

In fact, most of the women highlighted in this book took the
educational ride to discover their niche. While most of them
initially went to work in a field or industry related to their
bachelor's degree, few of them ultimately reached the apex of their
careers in those areas. Only one, Nancy Agee, had a calling—in
nursing—and obtained both her undergraduate and graduate
degrees in that area.

On the flip side, college is not for everyone and should not be
viewed as a prerequisite for achieving success in life. While Wendy
Johnson attended one of the top-rated university systems in
America, she did not graduate from college. Yet, she served as the
president and CEO of one of the most respected leadership and

communications training organizations in the world for nearly two decades.

It is common for an MBA to be listed as "preferred" or "strongly recommended" for those seeking roles in senior management. As Garry Ridge, chairman and CEO of the WD-40 Company, said in my first book, *The WOW Factor Workplace*, it can "confirm what you think you know and enable you to learn what you don't know," about business management. Yet, while an MBA can certainly be a benefit to anyone in leadership, having one is not generally a firm requirement. Just two of the executives highlighted in this book obtained an MBA.

Aside from certain professions—such as in scientific engineering, medicine, or for university professors

While an MBA can certainly be a benefit to anyone in leadership, having one is not generally a firm requirement. Just two of the executives highlighted in this book obtained an MBA.

—a PhD is rarely required. To the contrary, in some business cultures, a PhD could be a detriment. I have known some hiring managers to discredit candidates with a PhD, as potentially too focused on theory versus having a bias for action.

The one thing all of our women on top seem to have in common is that, when they decided to go to college, they were career focused. Each had an objective to earn a living by pursuing something they enjoyed doing. While it took some of them a while to find that special something, they passionately pursued whatever that was to the best of their ability once they found it. In my opinion, too many people use higher education—having a particular degree or the lack thereof—as an excuse for not going after what they really want to do in life.

> **In my opinion, too many people use higher education—having a particular degree or the lack thereof—as an excuse for not going after what they really want to do in life.**

If obtaining a particular degree is indeed a requirement, or even if it is simply something you would like to do and you can afford the investment, then go for it. But never let higher education, or the lack thereof, keep you from executive leadership.

INTROSPECTIONS:

1   Did you (or do you) have a career calling? If so, did you (or are you planning to) pursue that calling? Why or why not?

2   If you have a college degree:
- Did you consider your career path before you selected a major?
- Did your degree give you more self-confidence, or do you believe having it has accelerated your advancement? Why or why not?
- Was the investment to obtain your degree, in terms of your time and money, worth it? Why or why not?
- What did you learn in college that has most impacted your career journey?

3   If you do not have a college degree:
- Could a degree make a difference to your career success? Why or why not?
- If you were to obtain a degree, what would you major in and why?

4   If you could do college or grad school over again, what would you do differently?

FOUR

The Value of Your Personal Brand

You must spend some time understanding what your value is to the organization. Then, do not keep that a secret. That is not how the world works.

-LINDA RUTHERFORD
Senior Vice President, Chief Communications Officer, Southwest Airlines

W ell into my corporate career, my vice president boss, Todd, said to me, "Do you realize how, whenever you walk into a room, all heads turn to you? Everyone is dying to hear what you have to say."

My immediate response was, "I've never noticed that." What I was really thinking was, *You've got to be kidding me!* Then, however, I realized it must be true or he would not have said it. Sometimes other people can see the value of our personal brands better than we can.

Todd gave me quite a compliment, yet his message came as a complete surprise. No matter how confident I seemed to everyone else, inside I felt as though I had to prove myself anew, every day. In retrospect, it was sad that I did not fully appreciate the fact that I had already proven myself.

Isn't it interesting how easy it can be to see how capable other people are, yet how difficult it can be to see the same qualities in ourselves?

Successful leaders generally possess at least some awareness of the unique value they have to offer. If you are self-aware enough to realize this about yourself, do not be reluctant to let those above you know what you can do for the organization.

On the other hand, no matter how fantastic your "WOW Factor" workplace may be, and no matter how heartfelt your current manager is, never assume anyone, not even your best-ever boss, is looking out for you and your career. It is one thing for you to do great work every day, but it is quite another thing to ensure the powers that be understand your career goals and are actively engaged in helping you get there.

Never assume you will magically be offered a great promotion the next time the perfect stretch opportunity for you appears on the horizon. While you may have been offered your first promotion or two seemingly out of the blue, promotions are not automatically bestowed upon you once you reach mid-level management. You must take charge to lead your own career mission from the front. It is up to you to make your value known to the key decision-makers by planting those seeds with clarity and specificity.

Articulating the value of your personal brand is not the same thing as bragging. It is simply letting someone higher up, who may not be aware of your accomplishments, know your ideas

It is up to you to make your value known to the key decision-makers by planting those seeds with clarity and specificity.

about how you could lead the effort to move the organization ahead and why you can be trusted to make things happen. Your ability to do so is vital to your success.

If the right people have not noticed or do not appreciate your best efforts, those efforts may be meaningless. Those above you need to be made aware that you are ready, willing, and quite able to take that next big, important, career-broadening step.

If you are unsure about the value of your personal brand, ask those who know you well to be candid with you. How would they define your brand? What do they think you are especially adept at?

Understand that different people may view your value differently, depending on how they know you. I am quite sure my boss Todd saw my value in ways that were different from how my best friend from college might. So be sure to seek input and insights from those who know you from a job performance and career potential perspective.

Valuing Yourself Is Not Bragging

When I founded my leadership development firm some years ago, we placed a major emphasis on helping the women in our programs define their brands and articulate their value—without thinking of this as "bragging." I found it interesting that most of these women could easily define what they believed to be the value propositions of their direct reports. Most could even articulate

their own value

> **Regardless of their level on the leadership ladder, few [women] were able to explain why someone should consider them for their next desired position.**
>
> **Men rarely seem to have this problem.**

propositions in previous roles. Yet, regardless of their level on the

leadership ladder, few were able to explain why someone should consider them for their next desired position.

Men, on the other hand, rarely seem to have this problem.

I have dialogued with various executives about this phenomenon—how men and women balance humility and confidence differently. Some say it is because little girls are raised to be nice versus aggressive. Later, when they grow up, women wonder whether it is "nice" to think highly of themselves.

One executive I know serves as a mentor to women attending an executive MBA program. She challenges the female MBA students to write down what they believe is their unique value proposition—and to love the words they use. In doing so, not only do they become more self-aware and accepting of their brand, but they also gain much-needed confidence in terms of verbally describing what they could uniquely offer in their desired next position.

I can personally attest to the fact that for many women, this is an ongoing career struggle. My suggestion is this: Every time you accept a promotion and develop new skills, take the time to reassess whatever you have learned lately and what you can now do for a particular organization. Learn to appreciate whatever it is that you have most recently added to your professional skills repertoire and

Never let articulating the value of your personal brand—what only you can do so well for others because you are who you are—keep you from executive leadership.

acknowledge how these new experiences, along with everything else you have done, could benefit another organization.

The fact is, you never "arrive." Life is a continuous journey. There is no ultimate destination, even after you retire. So, keep putting yourself out there and humbly wear your personal brand as a badge of honor, as long as you live.

While it may be easier said than done, you simply need to harness the confidence that others have in you. Never let articulating the value of your personal brand—what only you can do so well for others because you are who you are—keep you from executive leadership.

Melissa Reiff
Former Chairwoman and CEO
The Container Store

When I interviewed Melissa Reiff in The Container Store's Coppell, Texas, headquarters, I brought up, "One of the things I hear all the time is, 'You must be able to articulate your value to get promoted to the next level.' Have you ever felt the need to do that?"

I have never asked for a raise. Never. I just did not. I always felt that if I surrounded myself with good and fair people, they would recognize my value and contributions and reward me appropriately.

Yes, it all worked out for me; however, I do feel that if you do *not* feel you are being compensated appropriately, you absolutely should speak up—and of course, the way you do so is important.

"Did you ever ask for a promotion?"

Not really, but it is a new day. It is a brand-new day.

I don't know. Maybe I should have spoken up and articulated my desires more. I do think about that sometimes. Sheryl Sandberg, in her book *Lean In,* and other women as well, do speak out about how, as women, we must speak up more. We must stand up for ourselves to make sure we are treated equally.

I most certainly believe that. Frankly, I was taught by my parents to do just that.

I guess I never felt that I had to.

Jodi Berg
President and CEO
Vita-Mix Corporation

Jodi Berg, PhD, shared this story about how she finally came to have confidence in the value of her personal brand:

> While I was working at the Ritz-Carlton—after I got my MBA and before I came back to the family business—a light bulb came on.
>
> When you are passionate about something all the fear that we have about putting ourselves out there becomes irrelevant. The reason we are putting ourselves out there is very different. It is no longer, "I've been asked to speak and what are these people going to think about me?"
>
> Instead, your lens becomes, "All of these people are here because they want to understand something differently. I can help them get there. I am here for them. They are not judging me. They want to learn something."
>
> I ended up becoming a good public speaker. The vice president of the Ritz-Carlton, who was traveling all over the world talking about the Malcolm Baldrige National Quality Award, heard me speak one time at the local property. He started calling me to be his substitute speaker.

When I was traveling all over the world, talking about the Ritz-Carlton and quality, was when I found my third love, international.

Start over is relative. At what point would you be restarting? I am a firm believer that we cannot go back. We can only apply and adjust continuously as we go.

Eventually an opportunity opened up for me to serve and improve systems and processes on an international level. It was this opportunity that brought me back to the family business as their director of international.

I asked Jodi, "Is there anything you would do differently if you could go back and start over?"

That is interesting. I do not know. *Start over* is relative. At what point would you be restarting? I am a firm believer that we cannot go back. We can only apply and adjust continuously as we go.

One thing I would say is this: If I could have adjusted sooner, I wish I could have recognized sooner what I recognized after having a near-death experience.

If I had only known earlier, *I have value!* It took me to the age of 30—seeing my life flash before my eyes—to realize, *I've got something I can add.*

If I had only known earlier, *I have value!* It took me to the age of 30—seeing my life flash before my eyes—to realize, *I've got something I can add.*

Nancy Howell Agee
President and CEO
Carilion Clinic

Nancy Agee had this to say about her own level of self-confidence, and how she views her value to the organization she leads.

> I do not mean to say that I am reckless, but I might be more prone to ask for forgiveness than ask for permission.

To that, I responded, "Have you always been that way, or did that personal characteristic develop over time?"

I think most leaders have a confidence gene in them. So, it is a gene that

The turtle is my favorite animal. The reason is—there are a lot of things you could say about turtles, but the fact is—she cannot get anywhere unless she sticks her neck out.

needs splitting, right? It needs honing. I started to say it is a skill, but confidence is not a skill. You become more and more confident over time.

This is not exactly an urban myth, but I have a little brass turtle sitting here on my desk. The turtle is my favorite animal. The reason is—there are a lot of things you could say about turtles, but the fact is—she cannot get anywhere unless she sticks her neck out.

The other one that is quintessential is: When you see a turtle on top of a fence post, you may wonder, *How did she get there?*

You know she did not get there by herself.

So, I have my little turtle here. Somebody gave it to me quite a long time ago. My roommate in nursing school and I both had turtles. We had two turtles. We could not have animals in our dorm, but we got these two turtles and we kept them for almost three years. I think we just wanted to have something living and different. But it came to be a symbol of how I think. It reflects my personal philosophy.

"Throughout your career, when you saw things you wanted to do, it seems you just went after them. Did you ever feel the need to articulate your value, or did you simply have enough self-confidence to go in and ask for whatever it was that you wanted?"

I think women are not socialized to display self-confidence, sometimes.

I have seen a great example, and I mention this to the women I mentor. I will ask them, "How often do you go up to shake someone's hand and initiate, 'Hello. My name is…'?"

Most of the time, if you watch around a room, it is not the women who work the room. Women seem a little hesitant. I am always surprised at that. So, I tell women, "Practice saying, 'Hello. My name is…' and make your two-minute talk, your elevator pitch about yourself."

Men seem more comfortable with that, I think.

In terms of articulating value, I think you must start with the
initial impressions we make. But I must admit, that has not
been my problem.

I replied, "I understand that your grandmother encouraged you
early in life by saying, 'It's okay to fail, but it's not okay to not try.'
Do you think that made a difference?"

Oh, I do. I do. That voice is in my head, still to this day.

Linda Rutherford
Senior Vice President, Chief Communications Officer
Southwest Airlines

When I spoke with Linda Rutherford, I shared with her that many
of the female executives I have spoken to have told me the story
about how a typical guy, who maybe meets only 30 percent of the
requirements, will say, "I can do that job. Put me in there!" Yet,
women tend think they must meet 100 percent of the
requirements to be qualified. Similarly, some women will say, "I
am excellent at what I do. I should be the next one promoted," yet,
they won't go and ask for the promotion. Instead, they are stunned
when a less-qualified guy gets the promotion.

I asked Linda, "What's your advice to women who think that is
happening to them?"

I think you must spend some time deciding what your personal brand is.

Are you a fixer? Are you a problem-solver? Are you a connector? Are you a collaborator? Are you a thinker?

You must spend some time understanding what your value is to the organization. Then, do not keep that a secret. That is not how the world works.

As women, we must raise our hand. We must be able to articulate what our personal brand is along with the value we bring to the organization.

At least in our organization, culturally, we all work together. There is a lot of vulnerability in our teamwork dynamic. You must be able to say what you are good at and admit what you are not good at. That way we can all figure it out and fill in the gaps.

I agree that one of the things we, as women, do is: We go heads-down. We try to do a good job and then we just wait to get noticed. I do not think that anyone can just wait to get noticed. I think sometimes women tend to work that way. For some reason, we think, *If they can just see how diligent I am, how hardworking I am, and see what a great work ethic I have, I'm going to get selected.*

We must be more organized and intentional about it and decide what our personal brand is. Then we must make sure the people we work with know what that is. Just say, "I can help here because I can do this. This is something I'm good at." That is how you make sure you are developing those relationships, so people come to depend on you for those things that are strong in your personal brand.

Next, I asked Linda to share why she thinks women may be reluctant to articulate their personal value.

> I was talking to a friend of mine who is a political researcher. He was telling me that women do not enter politics at the same ratio that men do.

> He thinks it is because, just as you mentioned, a man will step

A man will step up and interview for a role for which he might be only 60 percent qualified, but a woman must feel 110 percent qualified before she will put herself out there.

> up and interview for a role for which he might be only 60 percent qualified, but a woman must feel 110 percent qualified before she will put herself out there. He was making that analogy into politics, that women will not put themselves out there because they fear they are not qualified enough.

> I thought that was interesting. For whatever reasons, in the back of our brains, we stop ourselves. We should not do that.

I commented, "I've never seen any research that explains why women have that tendency."

> I have not either. But he has the research that shows that women are not generally entering politics. Then look what happens. You have seen some of the brand-new female freshmen congressmen and what they have been called. I mean, why would you subject yourself to that kind of criticism?

I applaud their bravery. But I do not think society is always friendly to outspoken women.

Kerry Healey
Inaugural President
Milken Center for Advancing the American Dream

When I interviewed Kerry Healey, PhD, who is a former lieutenant governor of Massachusetts, I commented, "When you ran for office, you had to sell yourself and the value of your brand. You had to clearly describe what you intended to do for people, right?"

Yes, but women usually run for office because they care about a cause, and it was the same for me. I do not want to generalize too much about how "all women do this, or all women do that." But, nearly half of women who run for office do so because they are moved by a cause. It is not about them as individuals, by and large.

Maybe there is some issue in their neighborhood. Maybe there has been an illness in their family. Maybe they care about their kids' school. There is usually a personal connection, I find, between women's stories about why they run for office and the causes that animate them—the causes that have created this passion that is so strong that they are willing to take the personal risks associated with being out there in public life.

I am not sure that it is the same for male candidates. Many male candidates simply believe that they are good leaders, and they will deal with whatever issues come along. It is much less frequent that you will hear a man say, "I'm running for office because I care about the environment, or I care about education, or I care about healthcare."

Instead, they say, "I am running because I have the qualities necessary to lead."

Like a lot of women, I too tend to dodge the questions requiring me to explain my personal value. Instead, I refocus the discussion on those things that I care about and that I want to change.

Next, I asked Kerry, "How was it that you became president of Babson College?"

I was recruited for the position.

"Certainly, you had to articulate your value to them in regard to what you could do for the university."

Well, interestingly, it was almost the other way around.

I had not even considered going into higher education. But then I was called by a recruiter, and I was intrigued. When I met with the selection committee, I was very curious as to why they thought I would be a good leader for the college.

It was a case of them explaining to me that they were a college focused on entrepreneurship, and they viewed my life as having been entrepreneurial.

I asked, "So you got them to articulate how they viewed your value to you?"

Honestly, I did not necessarily see my value in the same way they did. They had seen the policy innovations I had worked on, including healthcare reform, starting my little TV business that did not go anywhere, and launching a nonprofit in Afghanistan that educated Afghan lawyers and judges as entrepreneurial ventures. I had always just considered them to be some very disjointed things that I had done in my life.

They saw how my passions were connected. I had always wondered why I could not just settle on a certain course and do one thing. Ultimately, I realized that their perspective on my life was correct.

Thanks to that interview process, I began to see myself differently. I came to understand, for the first time, how running a nonprofit in Afghanistan and starting a television show and being engaged in politics could all be connected on some basic level—I was looking for ways to create positive change.

It is why *an entrepreneurial mindset* is now one of the pillars that we work on at the Milken Center for Advancing the American Dream. I think many people, when they hear the word *entrepreneur,* think of starting a business. That's quite often what it is. But it can also be a mindset that allows you to be a problem-solver across many different platforms—for-profit, nonprofit, volunteer, or whatever you are doing.

Babson really helped me to see myself as an entrepreneur. But nonetheless, I still do have a hard time talking about what my value is.

To that I commented, "So you're not that different from other women."

No.

"When you subsequently interviewed to lead the launch of the Milken Center for Advancing the American Dream, did they tell you what they saw as your value, or did you do a little more selling this time?"

I was doing a little more selling. But I think that by this time in my career, I am very fortunate that people call me, instead of me calling them. I took the approach that I would see where life took me.

I was in my sixth year at Babson. I had completed two terms as president. We had celebrated our centennial. I had raised the money I wanted to raise and built the buildings I wanted to build.

As I was about to turn 60, I wanted to start a new chapter in my life. So, I simply let it be known that I was going to step down from Babson in a year, and I literally gave myself a year to talk to anyone who wanted to talk to me. And I think that is the key point here. I was willing

I was willing to consider opportunities way outside my comfort zone or experience. Later in your career, you just have to have the confidence that you can learn new skills as required.

to consider opportunities way outside my comfort zone or experience. Later in your career, you just have to have the confidence that you can learn new skills as required.

There were a very diverse set of opportunities presented, and I am glad that I landed where I did.

Wendy Johnson
Former President and CEO
Dale Carnegie franchise, Atlanta, GA

When I interviewed Wendy Johnson, I mentioned that while I was running the peer mentoring programs for my leadership development firm, we found that women were not as adept or as comfortable as men in terms of articulating the value they deliver to their organizations. I commented, "Throughout my career, I have found guys, in general, are much better at telling others what they've done for the team. Women just don't seem to do that."

You are right.

We have found women do not communicate important information about themselves—things hiring managers really should know—when they interview for a job.

Women just wonder why the person who brags about himself all the time gets the promotion. They'll say, "That guy is such a braggart. How could they promote him? He's so cheesy."

When they do not get promoted, it is not that they do not deserve it, but they generally haven't talked themselves up to those who need to hear it. Often, they have not asked for the promotion.

Similarly, we have found women do not communicate important information about themselves—things hiring managers really should know—when they interview for a job. They will come home from the interview and their husband or parent will say, "How did it go?"

They will say, "Well, I think it went pretty well."

"Did you tell them that you were chosen by the governor for a special leadership program in Augusta this year?"

"Well, no."

"Why didn't you tell them that?"

"Well, because they didn't ask me."

By not proactively sharing such things, women undermine themselves. They do not know how to present their brand. They do not want to brag.

I replied, "When preparing for an interview, or anytime you are interested in getting a better job, you need to think about what the interviewer needs to know about you. If they do not ask you something, you need to find a way to fit your remarkable accomplishments into the conversation. You must distinguish yourself from the others."

Exactly.

My daughter is still working at Dale Carnegie, running the Atlanta business development group. She interviews people all the time, and, unfortunately, there are so many who do not meet the mark.

But then, one day, this woman in her mid-20s came sailing through the front door of their office. It was a cold call! She walked straight in and said, "Hi! My name is Karen. I am interested in working for Dale Carnegie. Who would I talk to?"

This is shocking, right?

I replied, "Wow! I would immediately say to her, 'Come on in!' I would have interviewed her on the spot."

Well, Alex and her manager happened to be there alone, and they did say, "Come on into this office!"

In just five minutes, she got that job because she could sell herself. The power of that is so important.

The young woman said, "I'm a teacher. That was what I got my degree in. I think I am a good teacher, but that is not what I want to do. I want to work for Dale Carnegie. I want to be in sales. I want to interact with people. I want to help people," and she goes on and on and on.

Then she said, "When can I start?"

Now, this is so rare. My daughter and her manager just looked at each other and then they looked at her. It was like, "Where did you come from?"

I interjected, "I would have said, 'You can start right now!'" Yeah, "Just give me some references!"

Of course, Karen has been an absolute superstar ever since because she was confident, unafraid to take the risk of rejection, and she had courage.

She took a risk. In just five minutes, she got that job because she could sell herself. The power of that is so important.

Lieutenant General Kathleen M. Gainey
U.S. Army, Retired

When I interviewed Lt. Gen. Kathy Gainey, I inquired, "Did you ever have to sell yourself into a position or were you always pushed into positions?"

A little bit of both. Sometimes I was given opportunities where I was perhaps not the first choice for the organization, but somebody else had pushed my name forward.

Sometimes I would have to plant the seed of, 'I think I can command the Defense Distribution Center," but was told, "Well, we don't see that for you. We see these other three jobs as opportunities for you."

I would still let my bosses know, "I think I would be good at that other job, and here's why. Here is what I need to develop. I think that job would help broaden me."

By doing so, my bosses and mentors could plant the seed to help me get this other opportunity with the officers who were the decision-makers. So, I did get the Defense Distribution Center job, not because I was the number-one person on the list, but because other people had planted that seed. The decision-maker then said, "Okay, yeah. I guess we could put her in there if you think she can do it."

I was also selected to be the Joint Staff J4, not because anybody in the Army was nominating me, but because somebody from another branch of service said, "Hey, what about Gainey? I think she'd be good in that job."

"How did that happen, when someone in another branch of service nominated you for a position?"

It was because I had worked with the other branches of service in different joint jobs.

"Was there a point in your career when articulating your value became important in order for you to get promoted into a particular position?"

I think it was when I would explain to my boss, "I'm a good team-builder and I'm good with people, so here is the value I think I can offer this organization. Here's what I think I can bring to the table. What is it you want me to focus on?"

"Some people have a hard time articulating their value."

> Sure, because nobody wants to boast. So instead, you can talk about your value, not in terms of, "Here is what I do well," but, "Here is what I can help *your organization* do well "
>
> This way, it is not about you. It is about how you can help the organization. It is saying, "Here's what I can help *us* do."

REFLECTIONS:

No matter how successful some C-suite women—including CEOs—may be, it is not uncommon for them to struggle with articulating their value from time to time. While some can readily articulate their value in a role they have played for a while, it can be a challenge to do so for their next desired position, or when they suddenly find themselves in a role that is new to them or is a dramatic departure from anything they have done before.

On the other hand, some women on top got where they are by simply letting their contributions speak for themselves.

Here are some practical ways to increase your confidence in your own value proposition:

- Always do your best and surround yourself with others who value who you are, but do not just wait to get noticed.
- Ask your boss, your mentor, or another leader senior to you—people who know you from a professional standpoint—to describe how they see you.

- Intentionally spend time deciding what you want your personal brand to be, then do not keep it a secret. Be your own brand manager.
- Write down, in your own words, what you believe is your value proposition. Love the words you use to describe yourself.
- Practice your elevator pitch and be ready to use it when you attend networking events. If you stumble with it, you can always refine it next time.
- Proactively tell your boss and decision-makers higher up, "I can help the organization do this. This is something I am good at. I want to do this."

Push yourself to keep growing yet remain true to who you are.

- Push yourself to keep growing yet remain true to who you are.
- When made aware of a developmental opportunity, speak up to your boss. Let those above you plant the seed with others.
- Accept public speaking opportunities. Keep in mind, the audience is not judging you. They will see your value as helping them learn something new. You will gain more confidence with public speaking the more you do it.

Remember, life is a journey. Enjoy the ride.

INTROSPECTIONS:

1   How could you help your organization move closer to achieving its vision while simultaneously helping yourself move closer to achieving your own career objectives?

2   How would you define your personal brand?

3   How would you state your value proposition as a 30-second elevator pitch?

4   How does your personal value proposition distinguish you from everyone else?

5   Think about that next ideal job on your career ladder. How would you define your unique value proposition for the next role you are aiming for?

FIVE

Closing the Gaps

I can see stars with incredible clarity that others cannot. I need somebody who can help me create the telescope so others will now be able to see the stars that I see. I am not the telescope. I do not need one because I can see the stars without the telescope. I need somebody who can envision the stars out there, enough to know what type of telescope is needed, so that others can see that vision.

-JODI BERG, PHD
President and CEO, Vita-Mix Corporation

L ike it or not, we all have weaknesses. We all have at least a few things we do not naturally do as well, or as easily, as others. But how much time should we spend trying to shore up our weak points? In fact, is it even possible to develop an energy and passion for something you continually struggle to do?

When I was in elementary school, I remember my parents telling me, in a very loving way, "It really does not matter what your grades are, as long as you are doing the best you can."

But somewhere along the way, I discovered that if my report card for the semester did not reflect an "A" grade in every subject, my parents would express their concern that I might not be doing the best job possible. Their advice was usually akin to, "You should try harder next semester."

By the time I entered high school, I had learned to do whatever it took to achieve an "A" every time. I became obsessed with my grades and somehow managed to graduate at the top of my class in high school, college, and graduate school. Frankly, it was a lot of pressure to put oneself under.

It took me a while to realize it was not necessary to be the best at everything.

Yet, I learned what I was capable of. I also discovered there was a significant difference between my natural talents and the areas I consistently struggled with, in terms of my efficiency and effectiveness. I eventually learned to try to avoid those things I did not enjoy.

It took me a while to realize it was not necessary to be the best at everything. Fortune 100 companies like AT&T, where I went to work after grad school, sent their high potentials to leadership development training to help them overcome perceived deficiencies. Some of this training was eye-opening and helpful. Some was a complete waste of time, considering the opportunity cost of not further developing what one enjoys and naturally does well.

I will never forget the day, early in my management career, when one of my career mentors said to me, "Deb, you know you can delegate the things you don't like to do to other people on your team."

That advice caught me by surprise. I replied, "But the job description for my position says that X, Y, and Z are my responsibilities. I can't delegate those things."

My mentor gently said to me, "Deb, that job description simply outlines the areas you are responsible for. It does not say that you must do each of those things yourself. You can assign some of those things to other people on your team, assuming you have someone who is interested and might enjoy learning something new."

Not getting it, I pushed back with, "But that particular item is not fun at all. I would never ask someone else to do my drudge work for me. They might get fed up and quit."

My mentor chuckled and said, "It may surprise you, Deb, but there are people who actually like to do tasks like that. Some people might be delighted to take their skills in that area to a higher level. Just figure out who on your team loves doing that and delegate to them."

We All Have Different Strengths, Gifts, and Passions

That idea blew me away. Of course, now it all seems so obvious, but back then, I was clueless. I just assumed that everyone who worked in a particular functional area excelled in and derived energy from the same things I did. What an awakening it was to discover otherwise.

It might have been the biggest blessing of my leadership career to discover how to foster WOW factor team performance: Focus on building on each team member's natural strengths and passions, rather than investing in improving their deficits.

Focus on building on each team member's natural strengths and passions, rather than investing in improving their deficits.

On a more personal note, self-awareness is an important key to success. To be an effective leader, you must be brutally honest with yourself in terms of acknowledging your weaknesses, strengths, and passions. Only then can you truly understand and optimize the value of your personal brand.

As a hiring manager, I liked to ask job candidates about their weak points, not as a gotcha question, but to assess their level of self-awareness. It is not unusual for people to say they do not have any weaknesses. Some interviewees will tell you they can do anything. But truly self-aware people, and certainly the most effective leaders, will readily admit to the things they do not enjoy and to what does not come naturally to them.

While interviewing the women on top highlighted in this book, I was eager to discover the areas in which they each felt weak. I wanted to learn how they handled closing those gaps. I hope you find their insights enlightening.

Melissa Reiff
Former Chairwoman and CEO
The Container Store

I asked Melissa Reiff, "What have been some of the biggest career development challenges you have had to deal with?"

Hmmm. Career challenges? Well, I think talent—finding and hiring great people—is always a challenge. As we always say, "You don't bat 1,000 with personnel."

Through the years, our company has been smart and intuitive. We use our good judgment as best as possible, and we will take calculated risks when we need to, weighing the risk and the reward.

Conducting an interview, or a "visit" as I like to refer to it, can be challenging. It is hard to discern if an individual s right for the team—for the company. But we all do the best we can.

We do have a bit of a reputation for asking candidates to "visit" with several people, not just one or two individuals. Truly, it is for one reason only. We have a responsibility with every candidate to make sure that we are communicating as much about our company and our expectations as possible, so the candidate is informed and feels confident in assessing the opportunity. It is their career, their work life. We should provide them with as much information about the company as we can, and from several different perspectives, so they, too, can make an informed decision.

We have a responsibility with every candidate to make sure that we are communicating as much about our company and our expectations as possible, so the candidate is informed and feels confident in assessing the opportunity. It is their career, their work life.

In terms of my challenges or weaknesses, I certainly have many things I can improve upon. I think if you ask our company leadership team, whom I work very closely with, they would say that I ask a lot of questions—maybe too many. Now, whether that is really a weakness or not, I don't know.

"Perhaps asking for more information is better," I interjected.

Always! But you must realize that at some point you have got to make a decision, even if you have just 80 percent of the information. You must use your intuition, your experience, and your best judgment. I believe at least 90 percent of the time, you will make the right call.

You must use your intuition, your experience, and your best judgment. I believe at least 90 percent of the time, you will make the right call.

However, I do always try to listen to those around me and collaborate when I feel it is necessary, as I certainly do not have all the answers. But I feel it is important if someone does have a different opinion than I do to build their case, so to speak, as to why they are right—you cannot just say, "I disagree."

Why is that? Why do you disagree? Tell me more if you feel passionately that your opinion is the right one. And if it is, then we will go with yours.

We are not quite a $1 billion company yet. We are close, and we will get there soon. I just feel a tremendous responsibility to all stakeholders to make sure we are successfu. And I do love all aspects of leading and running a business—the bigger-picture strategic responsibilities as well as all the details. That is probably why I ask a lot of questions—to make sure I understand clearly—and why I feel I must, so that good decisions are made.

I care so much.

But it is not about me believing I know best. Rather, it is about wanting to ensure we utilize the right people—the right brains—when it comes to making the right decisions.

I believe our leadership team has a lot of autonomy. I want people to make decisions, make mistakes, test, and learn.

We have made so many changes in the last five years. It is quite phenomenal as I look back at those positive and necessary changes as well as our accomplishments. Certainly, we have made some mistakes, but all in all, we have persevered.

In fact, when I took the role as CEO, the company leadership team and I created a five-page document identifying our challenges, opportunities, goals, etc. At our most recent company leadership meeting, we reviewed this document again and we literally checked off the things that we had completed and/or changed.

It is gratifying and important, I think, for the team to acknowledge our successes as well as the things we must continue to work on.

Jodi Berg
President and CEO
Vita-Mix Corporation

During my conversation with Jodi Berg, PhD, I asked her how she dealt with any weaknesses she sees in herself. I specifically asked her: "What are those things that you know to walk away from because they are like kryptonite for you—things that are not your strengths? What are the things that will cause you to get somebody else involved to help you shore up that weakness?"

This is where I rely on other people who have what I call *enabling superpowers.* One of those things, for me, is having somebody else who can visualize all the rungs on the ladder, so we can get from where we are today to the vision of where I think we can go.

If I can articulate what my end vision is, that destination that I am seeing—maybe it is a long-distance sighting—and then if I can partner with somebody who is good at defining all the steps that must happen to get there, once that person can see that something that is far off in the distance, then that is uniting two different superpowers—mine and theirs—to help make that happen.

I can probably get 70 percent of the rungs of that ladder in place, but when you are missing a couple of rungs, it is difficult to make that leap. So, I rely on surrounding myself with people who can clearly understand all the steps and will say to me, "This is too big of a leap. We need to fill in the gap to get people from here to there."

Now, the *kryptonite* you had mentioned. That is that thing that just sucks all the energy out of

> **I rely on surrounding myself with people who can clearly understand all the steps and will say to me, "This is too big of a leap. We need to fill in the gap to get people from here to there."**

you. Creating the rungs on the ladder is not necessarily kryptonite for me. It's just a superpower that I don't have.

I would also say that a superpower may not necessarily feel like an incredibly positive thing. Oftentimes, when I have this vision of what is possible, yet I cannot articulate it in a way that other people can see it, I can feel like, "Well, maybe I don't know what I'm talking about."

If I have the self-doubt that maybe what I am envisioning is not possible after all, because I cannot seem to articulate it in a way that other people can see it, that is really frustrating to me. But if I can surround myself with people who will be open enough to let me keep talking about it and explore it enough, so then they can see that vision, then they can help me articulate it in a way that other people can also see it.

For example, I can see stars with incredible clarity that others cannot. I need somebody who can help me create the telescope so others will now be able to see the stars that I see. I am not the telescope. I do not need one because I can see the stars without the telescope. I need somebody who can envision the stars out there, enough to know what type of telescope is needed, so that others can see that vision.

Nancy Howell Agee
President and CEO
Carilion Clinic

During my conversation with Nancy Agee, I commented, "All of us have things that we do better than others and things that we *like* to do better than others. What are some of the things that you know are not your strengths, and how do you deal with them?"

My first language is not healthcare economics. Of the many things that a CEO needs to do, one is being sure that we have the financial strength and resilience to do what we can do. Healthcare economics is quite complicated.

One thing that I had to truly double-down on, and still do—since I became the CEO—is really understanding the economic levers. That would be the area where I have the least strength and need to work on.

Here is another thing that is interesting to me. When my son was going to college, I became more aware of a real deficit—or *weakness* may be the right word. My education and my experience are significantly tilted toward healthcare. Yet, I am

> **I have spent a lot of time grooming myself for broader understanding, being curious, and nurturing a passion for lifelong learning, which I suppose is part of leadership.**

in an environment now, as a business leader, where there is a much broader world. I do not have all that background.

Whether it is music or art or politics or history, they were not part of my experience or education in a formal way. So, I have spent a lot of time grooming myself for broader understanding, being curious, and nurturing a passion for lifelong learning, which I suppose is part of leadership.

Linda Rutherford
Senior Vice President, Chief Communications Officer
Southwest Airlines

I asked Linda Rutherford, "Have you had any significant career development challenges, and if so, how have you dealt with those issues?"

Yes, a couple of things. I started down a career path where I thought I was going to be that "patches on the jacket sleeves" journalist forever.

Then I had a career pivot. That was a development challenge. When I came into the public relations role, even at the coordinator entry level, I did not really know what public relations was. Writing news releases, the whole writing and editing process, pitching stories to reporters, handling crisis communication, has all been on-the-job learning for me. I just got thrown into the deep end and had to figure out how to swim, slowly, over time.

So, my first career development challenge was to learn the craft of public relations. Tangentially, I had some of it through my journalism curriculum, but I really had to learn the profession. That was the first one.

Then, when I had the chance to become a senior manager in the department, the challenge was about leading people.

As you know, journalism is the ultimate individual sport. That was how I was wired. You do your thing, you give it to an editor, they edit it, and then it gets published. The concept of *team* was a career development challenge for me—to rethink how, if we were going to get things done, and done well, it would be because the *team* succeeds. It is not about me. That was just a switch in orientation.

It was not just about my own work product anymore. Leadership is about what we create as a team and about developing other people. So that next career development challenge was learning aspects of leadership and learning to figure out how to create the spark in that person that could help him or her be successful and stay motivated. I call it the ability to motivate and inspire others.

> **If we were going to get things done, and done well, it would be because the *team* succeeds. It is not about me.**

What does that look like? It is not the same for everybody. I learned you must spend time figuring out what that looks like, because everybody is different. Each person is at a different place in their career, and they have different aspirations. I had to get dialed into that.

Then, most recently, in the last five to eight years, it has really been about business acumen. It was no longer about just being a good communicator. Even in the chief communications officer role, it was about being a good business advisor, understanding the business model, understanding the finances, understanding the corporate strategy, and what would bring it all to life. This was another challenge I had to get my arms around.

I realize that in the role I am in now, I am advising on business topics that sometimes have a communications element, or even a communications resolution, but not always.

To that I responded, "Sometimes people get promoted into management because they did a particular individual contributor job well. But that does not necessarily mean that person is going to be a great manager. Sometimes we stumble before we really get it. What was that like for you?"

There were certainly some learnings.

If you think about it, I was just one of the dogs in the pack. Then, suddenly, I became the leader of the pack. Some of my stumbling was because I did not change any behaviors.

If there was somebody in the group I liked to go to lunch with, I went.

Similarly, here at Southwest, we have non-revenue travel privileges. We use our airline privileges to travel on the weekends with coworkers who are friends. I did not change any of those behaviors.

I realized very quickly that was not going to work. The pack is always watching how you behave as the leader. They want to know that you are invested in *all* of them. But the behavior that I was showing was that I liked to have lunch with this person. I liked to travel with that person.

There could have been the perception of favoritism, or that I was more interested in my friends' development than in developing others on the team. It took about a year, but I finally realized that.

I literally had to make a list of behaviors I was going to change. I was going to have to either eat at my desk or I was going to have a scheduled rotation of lunches with every single person on the team. I had to tell the person I traveled with that I could not do that anymore.

> **The pack is always watching how you behave as the leader. They want to know that you are invested in *all* of them.**

I had difficult conversations with some coworkers, telling them it was going to look and feel different going forward. That change would not mean that I was not invested in them and their success, but the nature of our friendship had to change.

I interjected, "That could be challenging."

Every day.

There are people you gravitate toward because they think like you. I get energy from them.

I am a Myers-Briggs "E." I'm an extrovert, so I get energy from being with and collaborating with others. I get energy from other people who think like me because I can go on, I can riff, and it is energizing.

I still must be careful of that every single day, honestly. There are people I would gravitate toward. Even in my peer set now, I have to be careful that someone doesn't feel like I'm ignoring them, or that I'm not invested, or I'm not there as an advisor to them, just because our styles are a little different.

I have to be careful that someone doesn't feel like I'm ignoring them, or that I'm not invested, or I'm not there as an advisor to them, just because our styles are a little different.

I realized that back then. I have also come to realize it is something I must still work on constantly.

I asked, "Did you come to that realization on your own, or did someone on your staff point that out to you, or did you have coaching from your peers or those above you?"

All of the above.

I knew something was not right because I did not feel like I had the trust of everyone on the team. Finally, a team member confided in me that, "Hey, this is what your behavior looks like. The perception is this."

Then, my boss Ginger said, "Look, you can't do that. You have got to be invested in all these people. You must also be realistic about what they are capable of. Just because someone is a friend does not mean they are the person who should be next in line, or that they are ready for promotion. Maybe they have things they need to work on. Maybe somebody else is more ready for promotion."

All those things were good learning moments for me, in terms of developing my leadership style back then.

I also think I have a bias for action. I would argue that this can be a shadow weakness at times.

I remember one of my coworkers was getting ready to retire. We were having a deep conversation one day and she said, "That *ready, fire, aim* approach of yours doesn't always work."

She was right. I would say that eight out of ten times it does work. But I know I sometimes need to slow down. It is not just because there's a better way of doing something. It is so that other people can catch up and get on the bus—you know what I mean? I realize sometimes I can get too far out ahead of people, with my ability to move fast. I must be patient and make sure I have got everybody on the bus so we can all go together. So, I am always checking that, as well.

You had a question about how to manage those weaknesses. Honestly, I just need to admit it.

I know I am often wrong, but seldom in doubt. If we need to slow down because you think there might be something I need to consider in my thinking, you must get in front of me and say, "Woah. Stop a minute. Think about this."

So, I must admit it. That is just how I am wired. Once I am onto something, it does not mean that I think you are wrong. It just means I'm thinking, *Oh, this is it! Let's go! Let us solve this,* because I'm often wrong but seldom in doubt.

All this was a huge awakening for me. It was freeing, honestly, because I could not figure out how to articulate it. But my retiring coworker did.

Success, by the way, could be something that you look back on and go, "Man, nailed that!" Success can also be, "That was terrible. Don't ever do that again," but you still learned from it. I still see those situations as success. I do not get wrapped up in failure very often. There is just no time for it.

I responded, "You mean, you just have to learn from it and move on."

> I do not get wrapped up in failure very often. There is just no time for it.

That is right.

"There can be a very fine line between a strength and a weakness. A strength can become a weakness if focused on in excess."

Sure, because it creates a blind spot.

"Are there other blind spots or weakness areas that you must still work on?"

Oh, sure.

I am an ENTJ on the Myers-Briggs Type Indicator. That is somebody who is decisive, moves fast, is an intuitive thinker, works more from logic than feelings, is a list maker, and very organized.

What I am constantly learning, and I do it every single day, is that I am notorious for seeing an e-mail and I will immediately want to give that person the answer they are looking for, or some advice, or some direction. So, I will write the e-mail.

I have had to teach myself, and I do this every single day, to go back and look at the e-mail again, before I send it. Sometimes I have not bothered to say, "Deb...how's your mom?"

I am just trying to get it done.

Another one of the things that I still struggle with is that "T" (Thinking) part of my personality, where I am just logically moving through things. I must stop and consider other people's feelings more than I am naturally inclined to do, not because I do not care, but because I get in the zone and I am wanting to help. It is like Acts of Service, right?

That is one of my love languages. It is like, let me do this thing for you because I know you are waiting on me. I must consider those unwritten things, sometimes. Maybe somebody just needs to be checked on. Maybe I need to see how they are doing. For me, that is a daily thing to work on.

> **I must consider those unwritten things, sometimes. Maybe somebody just needs to be checked on.**

Kerry Healey
Inaugural President
Milken Center for Advancing the American Dream

I asked Kerry Healey, PhD, former lieutenant governor of Massachusetts, and former president of Babson College, "Are there things that you've struggled with along the way?"

Yes, absolutely.

I am an introvert by nature. Almost every path I've chosen has required an extraordinary degree of extroversion, or at least the appearance of extroversion. That's exhausting. It is not natural for me.

When headed into a work event with new people, I constantly have to remind myself, *Okay. I need to meet everyone in the room. I need to learn their names. I need to find out why they're here. I need to find out what they need and what they are interested in.*

To be effective and successful as a leader, you have to be outgoing and open. You have to assume that you're there to be met and to meet people. You have to assume that everyone wants to know you—which is, to my mind, not true! I need to make a conscious effort to project openness when, in fact, I am reserved. That is just my nature. I think we're born with these characteristics, so it's more work for some of us. But it's work that must be done.

What strikes me is, when I go in and out of leadership positions, I immediately go from always needing to sit in the front row and meet

I need to make a conscious effort to project openness when, in fact, I am reserved...so it's more work for some of us. But it's work that must be done.

everyone, to naturally sitting in the back row, talking to no one. It just happens like *that* [she said as she snapped her fingers]. The second I'm no longer officially in that position, I am so happy to be back in the back row again.

I replied, "I'm sure a lot of people can relate to that. But as a leader, you must be able to talk yourself into being this other character."

Look, they're both real. They're both real. I *can* take energy from being in a room and talking to people. Coming into it, I have the anxiety of, "I'd really rather sit in the back. I'd really like to be at home." Then, once I am there, it is good. And afterward, I am very excited that I met all these interesting people and that I could interact with them in some way. I always feel better *after* an event than I feel before it.

"Anything else you'd like to share about shoring up weaknesses?"

I would consider my terrible fear of the media to be one of my weaknesses, as well.

It was reinforced when I was at a press conference in the state house, early on. I was being interviewed by someone with one of those shoulder cameras. There was a huddle of people with shoulder cams. At that time, Governor Whitman—Christie Whitman from New Jersey—walked past. She was a much more important person than I was. So, all the cameras

swiveled to talk to her. Suddenly, one of them hit me—bam—
right on the head and knocked me down.

So, I developed this phobia, like an "Oh, NO! Cameras!
Dangerous!" kind of association. I have had to overcome that.

I replied, "I've often wondered how politicians deal with
journalists from the media who seem focused on tripping you up
with each question. I can imagine learning to effectively deal with
that can be quite a challenge."

You are correct. Honestly, it is all a matter of practice and
trying to put yourself in their shoes, to understand why
reporters are asking those "gotcha" questions.

They are looking for
news. It is unlikely that
they hold any personal
animus against you. They
are simply trying to do

> **It is all a matter of practice and
> trying to put yourself in their shoes,
> to understand why reporters are
> asking those "gotcha" questions.**

their job. Their job is to learn something new. If they just let
you answer the question in the way that you would like to,
they won't learn. It would not be newsworthy.

I think trying to understand where that person is coming from
and viewing them as a regular person is very helpful. Trying to
understand the perspective of the interviewer motivated me
to start a small television production company once I left
office so that I could literally put myself in the shoes of an
interviewer, and that experience has made me much more
comfortable on camera.

Wendy Johnson
Former President and CEO
Dale Carnegie franchise, Atlanta, GA

Wendy Johnson spoke about the Dale Carnegie program and its focus on developing a command presence, also referred to as an *executive presence.*

I remember one time, when I was trying to get into a large multi-national company to position our program, one of their male employees visited our website. He also happened to be the president of their Toastmasters group. I thought, *Okay, now I'm going to get in there and find out what's going on.*

So, I asked him to lunch. During our luncheon discussion, I asked him about his position. It did not take long for me to discover that he did not even have a business card. At that point, I realized he was in a lower-level position, but he was passionate about public speaking, so I made the best of it.

When I asked him about his job, he said to me, "I've just been promoted into a supervisory position in the finance department."

Then he said, "I am failing, and I am miserable. When I wake up every day, I do not even want to go. I am frightened and I am failing. My wife and I discussed it and we've decided that it's okay if I go back to tell my company, 'Here is your supervisory position back. I just cannot do it. I would rather be an individual contributor in the department.'"

I said to him, "Do not do that. No, no, no, no! They have identified that you have leadership potential. You *can* do this job. You just need training in leadership."

"Well, what kind of training will make me more confident?"

"The Dale Carnegie program. Warren Buffett is a big proponent of the Dale Carnegie program. If you Google him, you will see that Warren Buffett says, 'You won't go anywhere until you've taken the Dale Carnegie course,' because that is what he did when he was twenty-two or twenty-three years old, after graduating with his MBA from Columbia University. It gave him confidence and the ability to communicate."

"Okay."

"Your company will probably pay for it. Go ask your tuition assistance organization."

So, he immediately enrolled in our class and he started winning awards in the class right away. He took it so seriously that when he graduated from that class twelve weeks later, he won the highest award of achievement (from his classmates) for showing the greatest leadership in the class. He became more confident in his job and he got another promotion!

After that, he came to me and said, "I want to be a Dale Carnegie instructor. This program has done so much for me. I want to empower others."

So, he went through the instructor's class—it takes almost two years to become a certified Dale Carnegie instructor. He became an instructor as he continued to be promoted at his company. His next promotion took him to Spain for an associate director position in auditing.

His success story really captures the essence of the importance of developing an executive presence. Now that was a guy, versus a woman, but these kinds of things happen for women all the time, too. We have learned that it is all about how people perceive you.

If a woman is not being promoted, and she feels she deserves it, she needs to do some self-evaluation. Women can blame the promotion challenge on men and discrimination, but it is not just that. There are always other factors. It can be an executive presence issue. Are you communicating? Do you have a voice? Do people perceive that you will follow up?

We recommend people take a personal assessment to identify their areas of strength and areas of weakness. There are assessments that help identify how others perceive us. This is where we discover our blind spots. If we do not know what our blind spots are, we are unaware of the areas that we need to develop.

Bottom line, we recommend that you find a coach or a mentor and get an assessment. Then, attend a training program that will enable you to fill the gaps.

The issue holding you back may not be public speaking or communication. It may be organizational skills or problem-solving skills. It may be something else. Who knows what it may be? Everybody has their own area that is holding them back from creating an executive image, an executive presence.

It is interesting to discover what people do not realize about themselves, especially if they were born and raised to be very polite. In the South, for example, they could have been taught as kids to be quiet, to be polite, and to not interrupt. These are all wonderful qualities that Southern people and others have, too. But what happens when you never speak up is that other people may think you do not have any ideas.

One thing that is hard to cure is being thin-skinned. If you think you have a self-confidence issue, or gaps in soft skills, or even in your

Everybody has their own area that is holding them back from creating an executive image, an executive presence.

technical ability, be proactive about getting some help with it. Hiring a coach is a wonderful solution because you have an advocate who is not within your peer group.

Now, as for my weaknesses: I am overly emotional, and I am Italian.

I responded, "Being Italian is not a weakness."

Oh, there is a flash point with Italians. You have got to be careful, right?

I can take things personally sometimes. That can make it difficult in business. Women are more prone to this.

When things get stressful and I do not feel in control, I have found that doing yoga or meditation can be effective to help reduce stress and anxiety. Any type of emotional and disagreeable response is unproductive.

Another weakness is that I can get a little too close to people. In leadership, you must be careful about how close you get, because you can cross a line when you have a personal relationship. You know too much about them.

> **In leadership, you must be careful about how close you get [to people], because you can cross a line when you have a personal relationship.**

Then, when it comes time for you to make a tough decision that you know will negatively affect that person, it can be difficult. You have made life harder for yourself. So, there must be a little bit of coolness there. Sometimes I violate that.

Lieutenant General Kathleen M. Gainey
U.S. Army, Retired

I asked Lt. Gen. Kathy Gainey, "With all those people who were watching out for you along the way, suggesting promotional opportunities, were they also trying to help you shore up perceived deficiencies?"

Yes, they were trying to help. One boss quickly realized I had terrible written communication skills—bad grammar, terrible spelling skills, and I could not write concisely. So, he really worked with me on that by making me rewrite many correspondences.

I do not think I even thought about my strengths and weaknesses, but I knew I was dyslexic. I knew that was an issue for me, especially when I had to enter the radio frequency and decode messages. I would reverse things. I had to be very careful and really pay attention to detail.

I think one of my weaknesses was that I did not understand many aspects of the military. You think you do, but you do not. I really had to ask a lot of questions. That may have bothered people but, fortunately, they were willing to bear through it and let me ask all my questions.

I think another one of my weaknesses was time management. I knew that from college. Sometimes I would get into a crunch time with an exam or a paper. I would wonder, *How did I get into this situation?*

So, I really started trying to think about, *Okay, what are the tasks? When do I need to do what?*

I would then try to block time to make myself do that, to create an internal suspense list, so that I would not get into those crunch times and not get things done.

Over time, you gain knowledge about other weaknesses that you did not even know you had, like not dealing well with confrontation; not wanting to attack a situation; maybe being a little too hesitant. You realize, over time, you have additional weaknesses.

I commented, "Maybe as we mature, we become more self-aware. Leaders must be very self-aware. How did you deal with the weaknesses that you realized later?"

First, in terms of taking on a project—picking it apart, figuring out the key actions that needed to happen, and then identifying how to schedule time for all that—I learned about the importance of blocking time on my calendar. I had to create that internal suspense list, put those things on my calendar, force myself into that process of checking, and make sure that I was making progress against whatever the goal was.

I had to create that internal suspense list, put those things on my calendar, force myself into that process of checking, and make sure that I was making progress against whatever the goal was.

"So, you found a way to make it work for you. In the military, could you delegate things to others, the way civilians or corporate managers would do, or did you have to bully your way through and figure out ways to solve issues on your own?"

I was able to delegate things to others. I often would surround myself with people who had the skill sets that I did not have.

As I said earlier, I am lousy at spelling. I am lousy at grammar. So, my administrative assistants had to be very strong at spelling and grammar.

I know I am not a good time manager. So, I would ask whoever was running my operations to lay out the timelines for what we were going to be doing and identify the key suspense points. I would say, "You create the plan, because I'm not going to be thinking about all that."

Also, I am not a strategic thinker.

To that I responded, "It's interesting to hear you say that. While I was running my leadership development firm, I quickly became aware that women are routinely discredited—in terms of being evaluated for leadership potential—for not displaying strategic competency. We would encourage the members of our program to use phrases like 'My strategy is…' or 'My vision is…' when speaking to others in the organization.

"I'm sure some folks might wonder how you became a lieutenant general when strategic thinking was not one of your greatest strengths. How did you overcome that?"

> I had to determine who the smart, strategic thinkers were. You can pull in the strategic skills of the people around you and empower them.
>
> You can say, "I need you to think long-range. You be the one to develop the strategy, because I am not a strategic thinker. I am a problem-solver, but I am not a strategic thinker. So, you are going to have to be my strategic thinker. You come up with the big ideas, and we can talk through them. I can help you with ideas and vectors, but you are going to have to be the one to get me out of my comfort zone. Otherwise, I am going to be sitting over there, just doing the status quo."

REFLECTIONS:

Executive-level leaders are typically quite self-aware. They know their strengths, acknowledge their weaknesses, and are not afraid to admit their shortcomings. When asked, each of the women interviewed in this book easily identified her stumbling blocks or "opportunities." They were also quite willing to share how they have managed to close any gaps.

Personal behaviors—such as showing favoritism toward certain team members, being overly shy or quick to anger, or having a fear of the media—can be overcome only by the individual herself. My experience working with high-potential women at all levels indicates that the need to overcome an undesirable character trait or two is common. No one is perfect.

Eventually, most high-potential women learn to modify such behaviors through coaching and focused attention, once the issue has been pointed out and acknowledged. Of course, overcoming such issues can be a critical success factor for anyone wishing to advance their career. Failure to correct behavioral challenges can stifle one's progression, if not derail one's career.

On the other hand, leaders who struggle to master needed expertise within a given functional area, or when certain tasks "suck all the energy out" of them—as Jodi Berg referred to it—may find delegation of such functions to be the quickest and most effective fix. Why struggle doing something that someone else far more capable can do for you?

Why struggle doing something that someone else far more capable can do for you?

Half of our women on top admitted to struggling with at least one functional area that is typically considered a prerequisite for serving in the C-suite—strategic vision and financial management. In each case, the executive simply surrounded herself with others more capable in the given functional area. Essentially, delegating those aspects of their job is how they closed those gaps.

INTROSPECTIONS:

1   What do you consider to be your primary areas of weakness? Be honest with yourself.

2   Have any of these weaknesses or blind spots inhibited your upward mobility? If so, what might you do to overcome such issues?

3   Do you have a manager, a mentor, a trusted peer, or a coach who could offer advice on how you might close these gaps? If not, think about who else you might reach out to for help and guidance.

4   Do you struggle with delegating? If so, why do you think that is?

SIX

Cross-Functional Experience

The very first move I made…was to work every position within the company, except training. I registered people and learned the whole registrar system, accounting, sales, and so on. I came to know every single bit of the business, because I had, by then, learned how powerful it was when the people reporting to you knew that you could step in and do their job, and most importantly, they knew that you knew what they were up against.

-WENDY JOHNSON
Former President and CEO, Dale Carnegie franchise, Atlanta, GA

No matter what industry you're in, you are likely to find there is no typical pathway to the top. Some people might enjoy a meteoric rise along a single functional path, like climbing straight up the ladder within sales or engineering. Some people may advance from one leadership role to the next as they bounce from one functional area to another within the same firm. Others may choose to broaden their skills by hopping from industry to industry. Some do all of the above.

After obtaining my MBA, I spent nearly three decades in one industry: technology. I worked for a small number of companies during that time. When I began my corporate career in this industry, major corporations had what was referred to as "high-potential" programs. Anyone identified as a "hi-po" candidate would be singled out early on in their career. These candidates were recommended for assignments across the company—here, there, and everywhere. Some of it seemed nonsensical to me at the time, but I eventually came to understand the reason for it.

I became an entrepreneur in Fortune 100 clothing.

Most of my cross-functional expertise was gained leading organizations that served a variety of customers, across a plethora of industries, in different countries around the world. Each one had unique business challenges within a wide variety of functional areas, all of which I learned from.

To me, every customer situation was a new beginning. I was energized by the constant opportunity to learn, adapt, and solve problems that no one else had resolved or even recognized before. Status quo was not my thing.

After a certain point in my career, I created most of the organizations I led. I rarely had a position that someone else had held before. That was how I advanced my career. I became an entrepreneur in Fortune 100 clothing.

But not everyone is like me, nor should they be. For the sake of continuity and depth of knowledge, it is important that every business have at least some portion of its staff centered within specific functional areas, like finance, marketing, technology, and so forth. There must be some level of stability and depth of expertise to have a thriving, WOW factor, industry-leading business.

There is certainly no single best way to manage one's rise to the top. Taking risky assignments in different functional areas that you know little about is not for everybody. Some people are much more comfortable being the expert in a certain aspect of the business, and therefore manage their career by going up the vertical chain within their functional discipline. Others are much more interested in learning broadly.

Those who take on cross-functional assignments—while it can be risky and uncomfortable at times—will eventually find that it can be an effective and fulfilling way to manage their career. There will come a day when they are the ones with the broadest perspective of all because they took on all those different assignments across the organization. When they get to senior leadership, they have a perspective that no one else does. Their disparate career path eventually makes sense.

Clinging to Comfort Zones Costs Us

Whichever way you choose to advance your career, you should always invest in broadening your skills to increase your value to the organization. Like it or not, to be an effective leader, you must consistently push yourself beyond your comfort zone. Go after opportunities

Go after opportunities that will give you experience in areas you are not familiar with, either within or beyond your current functional area. Make it a priority to keep learning and growing.

that will give you experience in areas you are not familiar with, either within or beyond your current functional area. Make it a priority to keep learning and growing.

Keep in mind, cross-functional experience can be a great thing to have if you want to make it to the C-suite. If a promotional opportunity will broaden your expertise, go for it if it will allow you to play to your strengths and will provide the environmental conditions you want. Contrary to what my friend Cara did, at least check it out before you turn down such an opportunity.

Cara had an undergraduate degree in economics and an MBA from a top-tier university. Over the course of her twenty-year career, she was eventually recruited to a director of product management position by a global technology company. Cara told me that she looked forward to someday becoming a vice president within that business division, and she hoped to eventually promote into an executive-level position.

One day Cara's manager, Jim, told her about a senior director position that would be opening in another product division of the company. He suggested Cara put her name in for consideration. Cara replied, "But I don't know anything about that product. How could I possibly be qualified for that job?"

Jim assured her that he knew the senior leadership team over there. He believed with Cara's tenacity, she could get herself up to speed in no time and would do a great job for them. It could be a career-enhancing move for her.

Skeptical, Cara pushed back, assuming there were far more qualified candidates for that position. Somewhat exasperated, Jim suggested Cara ask human resources to send her the job description and the list of qualifications for the soon-to-be posted position. He promised to review it with her once she had a chance to look it over.

A few days later, Cara took the list of qualifications to Jim's office. She sat down and shook her head as she handed the list to Jim, stating, "There are ten very specific qualifications for this job. I meet only seven of them. No way am I qualified."

Jim leaned forward, looked Cara in the eyes, and replied, "Cara, I hope you will forgive my offensive language, but don't be such a woman about this." Shocked and insulted by his response, she replied, "What do you mean by that, Jim?"

"I mean," Jim started in, "if I had mentioned this promotional opportunity to any of the guys reporting to me—your peer product management directors—every one of them would have immediately espoused to be totally qualified, even if they met only three out of those ten items. Here, you meet seven out of the ten, yet you tell me you are not qualified."

About a month later, while Cara was attempting to learn more about the other product division, in preparation for putting her name in for consideration, the vice president of the other division announced that one of Cara's peer directors had been awarded the senior director position.

Even with the backing of her manager, Cara lost out on that promotional opportunity because she was reluctant to step outside of her comfort zone.

As I interviewed the seven women highlighted in this book, I asked those who had taken a cross-functional route about the benefits of changing career paths to get to the top.

Nancy Howell Agee
President and CEO
Carilion Clinic

I started by asking Carilion Clinic President and CEO Nancy Agee, "How did you go from being a nurse to being the chief operating officer? Was that one step or were there several steps in between?"

There were lots of steps in between.

I became a nursing director for a couple years and I had an unofficial mentor who was a physician colleague. We were both interested in oncology. We developed a grant proposal to the National Cancer Institute. We won the grant, and we needed a leader for the grant. The grant was for three years and was renewable, so that was a total of about five years.

I had not anticipated being in that position, but when we won the grant, I said, "You know, I'd like to lead this."

There was a bit of a competitive process, but I led that effort for five years. It was a great experience. We included four competing hospitals within the region and developed a lot of really interesting things.

It was a super experience. It gave me some national exposure, too, because there were thirteen other organizations that had similar grants. We met quarterly in different places across the country, and we learned from each other. So, I got a lot of exposure.

When the grant ended, I had theoretically *not been* in nursing for five years. I was

I wrote a job description for a new position and presented it to the organization...It made sense to them. It would be good for the organization, and it was good for me.

casting around for, "What do I do next? What does it look like?"

Some of my interests and passions were in leadership development and education. So, I wrote a job description for a new position and presented it to the organization. I said, "I'd like to do this. What do you think?"

They said, "Okay."

It made sense to them. It would be good for the organization, and it was good for me. So, that started the ball rolling.

Over time, I became a vice president, then a senior vice president—with fairly disparate responsibilities—which then parlayed into the chief operating officer, and then the chief executive officer.

Kerry Healey
Inaugural President
Milken Center for Advancing the American Dream

With her vast breadth of functional expertise, Kerry Healey, PhD, had this to say when I asked, "What have been some of the biggest career development challenges that you've had to deal with?"

I can give you several examples.

One came early on in my career. I was at a think tank where advancement hinged on the depth of your knowledge in a specialty. For example, I started out doing research around drug control policy. If I had wanted to become the top person at the company in that regard, I would have taken another, and another, and another research project focused on the topic.

But what I wanted to do was build broad-based knowledge. I wanted to see how things connected. So I was constantly asking for projects that were outside my field of expertise. I would have just spent a year, or two years, studying one particular thing. Then I'd say, "Okay, I really want to focus on something else now." And I'd be starting from zero again.

So, for about ten years, I was pretty much the lowest person on the totem pole, again, and again, and again. I would go from studying drugs, to gangs, to witness intimidation, to domestic violence, to child abuse and neglect, to recidivism, to reentry, etc. I was always a new learner.

I found that, over time, by being a broad-based learner, I built a much better framework than if I had gone deep in one area. There are some places, like science, where you have to go deep. I totally understand that.

But, for most social sciences, and certainly policy work, you do much better if you understand

I found that, over time, by being a broad-based learner, I built a much better framework than if I had gone deep in one area.

how social issues connect with each other. If you think of public policy as a car, and the car breaks down but you only know about wheels, you can talk about how to make a better wheel, but maybe it's the engine that's broken. You need to really figure out how it all works together before you can figure out how to best fix it.

For me, the decision to be a generalist allowed me later to become much more integrated and impactful in the way that I crafted public policy. I wasn't looking at one component of it alone. I was able to understand how poverty interacts with violence, and how that interacts with the educational system, and how that might interact with domestic violence or child abuse, and so on. What happens if you don t graduate from high school? How does that relate to drug abuse or other criminal activities? All of these things are linked on some level, or at least they interact with each other in society, in very complex ways.

I commented, "That applies in the business world, as well."

Absolutely! You have to understand every branch of whatever organization you are in, and all the different functions that you are providing.

Most recently, when I was the president at Babson College, I had to hire a chief marketing officer. But, I never studied marketing. Campaigns are definitely involved with marketing, but that's a different kind of marketing. And the world has moved toward online marketing and sales now, so it was a whole new field for me.

I remember thinking, *I'm not sure that I can add anything to this hiring process. I'm not sure that I can wrap my arms around this fast enough to be useful.*

But over time, I did. Now I am putting together a marketing group for my next venture and I feel more confident now, as a leader, because I have done it before. I can have something to say of value on that topic.

When you are a college president, you are not only providing a product—an education—you must worry about the quality of that education. You need to think about your brand value throughout the world. You must think about the life experience, the daily experience, of your students on campus. You must run dormitories. You must serve food. You must provide public safety. You must provide entertainment. And you need to suddenly become an architect because you must build buildings all over the place. You need to find ways to connect with a giant alumni group that has needs and wants to interact with you. You need to raise money, so you must be a fundraiser, as well. And you need to be the face of the college, in speeches, on television, you name it.

There is almost no end to the types of skill sets that you need to be effective as a leader of a university. It gives you a lot of practice in odd little niches that you would not necessarily think of.

For example, I was able to take the experience that I had at Babson, overseeing over $200 million worth of building over the course of my time there on campus, and bring it to my current position. Here we are, building this new, wonderful visitor's center dedicated to the American Dream, past, present, and future. We are renovating and restoring extraordinary, historic buildings. It is a large project. I am not worried, though, because I just did similar things at Babson.

Wendy Johnson
Former President and CEO
Dale Carnegie franchise, Atlanta, GA

I asked Wendy Johnson to share what it was like earlier in her career when she transitioned from selling aluminum for a Fortune 100 company, like Martin Marietta was at the time, to the financial services industry.

Well, I had to learn all about aluminum. I covered the Pacific Northwest and I had customers like irrigation companies and the airlines, like Boeing, and all the companies that were around Boeing, and all the metals that they were feeding into Boeing. I had manufacturing customers like Kenworth Trucks and Peterbilt Motors Company.

Then, after a few years on that assignment, they wanted me to move to St. Louis where I would have had to work out of my home. I just could not do that—work out of my home.

I asked, "They wanted to move you across country and then have you work from home, way back then?"

They wanted to give me an additional territory, so I would cover all the territory from Seattle to St. Louis.

But I was alone, and I just did not want to be in St Louis, working out of my home and calling on accounts in the industrial part of St. Louis. I did not think I could do it because it would be too lonely for me to work alone at home, in a new town.

So, I went on a search for a new industry. I was tired of studying the bend ratios and heat tolerances of aluminum. I wanted an industry that would be more applicable to my life.

So, I picked computing services in the financial industry. The whole financial industry and the computer's impact on it interested me. I knew that I could be more of a thought leader in that market.

I remarked, "You certainly took some very broad steps between industries and technologies."

Many of the career changes that I made were the result of other life changes. I moved back to San Francisco from Seattle. It was just completely starting over, basically. That was back when you could make a change in industry and start a new endeavor without an established Rolodex file of customer contacts.

Many of the career changes that I made were the result of other life changes. It was just completely starting over, basically.

I went to work for National Data Corporation, which was a computer services company in the financial and healthcare field. I learned about cash management and called on the treasury department within large companies.

This industry change allowed me to develop a more sophisticated and meaty focus. The financial industry required a more formal presence. I had to learn a great deal about finance and how computer services could impact the speed of collections and the availability of investment dollars in the treasury area of a business. I sold cash concentration services and wire transfer systems to banks, as well.

Then, my husband moved me to Atlanta. At that point, I decided to start my own business. So, I partnered with a small company out of San Francisco, selling a payroll tax and cash management product to companies. I did do that out of my house.

But then, my husband took a new life direction with somebody else, which was unfortunate. We split up and I had to focus on finding a more serious employment track. I remained in sales but moved into sales management.

I ended up in a medical company. I know this all sounds very disparate, but although it was a departure from the financial industry, I was still selling a service.

This medical company provided medical surveillance for engineering firms whose employees were cleaning up the planet. These engineering companies were contracted to clean up hazardous waste sites all over the world.

The U.S. government—actually, the Occupational Safety and Health Administration (OSHA)—required these employees to have a physical exam before they joined the company, then one every year, and then a final exam when they left the company. These medical records had to be stored for thirty years so they could assure that exposure to hazardous waste was not affecting the employees' health.

Our medical company managed that entire process for these engineering companies. We contracted with clinics all over the country, we managed all the physical exams, we provided OSHA certifications, and we stored all their data for thirty years. I did that for about eight years. This was when I made my move into management and became their VP of sales.

After those eight years, I spent another eight years with a banking consulting firm, Carreker Corporation, where I had a global sales management role, selling check and e-fraud detection software to banks all over the world. This is where I learned that international business has its own set of business rules, quite different from those in the United States. In the U.S., we tend to be fast and direct. Internationally, they do business like a ballet—smooth and measured. I had to learn patience and react more gracefully.

From all my experience in previous roles, the very first move I made when I bought the Dale Carnegie franchise in Atlanta was to work every position within the company, except

training. I
registered
people and
learned the
whole registrar

International business has its own set of business rules, quite different from those in the United States. In the U.S., we tend to be fast and direct. Internationally, they do business like a ballet—smooth and measured.

system, accounting, sales, and so on. I came to know every single bit of the business, because I had, by then, learned how powerful it was when the people reporting to you knew that you could step in and do their job, and most importantly, they knew that you knew what they were up against.

I replied, "I think what is so inspiring about your story, Wendy, is that you were always starting something new. That seems to be a common trait. Some of the best C-level leaders have done all kinds of things. Some of them never even aspired to be at the top, but suddenly they found that they were the most qualified to be at the top because they knew something about almost every aspect of the business."

Yes, that happens, and you can be very powerful when you get there.

Lieutenant General Kathleen M. Gainey
U.S. Army, Retired

Lt. Gen. Kathy Gainey had this to say about the benefits of having broad-based, cross-functional experience:

After serving as a company commander in the military, where you oversee anywhere from 100 to 200 people across a myriad of functions, you then become a staff officer, where you serve on somebody's staff and help to make things happen in a more specific functional area, but on a larger scale—at a battalion or a brigade. Or you might do as I did in a services organization like the military traffic management command, which is a military organization, but is pretty much civilian-run.

Then, after that, you might do a little bit of staff work at a higher-level organization, in strategy and policy, or in operations or training, because you now have a better understanding of the potential problems and challenges.

Then you just keep going up in rank, between staff and command assignments, as you continue up the officer ladder. It is always with increased authority and increased responsibility, sometimes with more people, sometimes with fewer people.

When I went to the documentation section for vessel and container loading, at the military traffic management command, we only had 35 civilians, but we had a very big mission of uploading all of the manual documentation into the computer system.

This was back in the day when we were just starting to use computers. Back then, you were entering the data as you loaded a ship or a container. We created an eighty-column punch card for each item. The exact location in the vessel was manually transcribed, and somebody had to type that in to create the eighty-column punch card. We then created the ship's manifest, which indicated all the contents loaded on the ship, the ultimate organization it was going to, and the location of that ultimate organization.

Today it's all electronic, and you scan it with a barcode. But, back in the day, it would be a crunch time because you were trying to load the ship with all these supplies and equipment, and then you were trying to build the manifest, because you had to have a physical manifest before the vessel sailed.

"What were some of the biggest career development challenges you had to deal with as a woman in the military?"

The biggest challenges were not so much about being a woman, but more about the fact that I was getting into fields that I knew nothing about.

When I went into the military traffic management command, suddenly I was learning how to deal with civilians. I was coming in and treating them like my soldiers. But you cannot order civilian people around.

I can remember a couple of people stopping and sitting and chatting. I said, "Hey, we've got a ship to load. Get back to work!"

"We're on our eye-break."

"Eye-break? We do not take eye-breaks. This is the military. Get back to work!"

Well, come to find out, *we did* have a negotiated agreement, a union labor agreement for the civilians. I didn't realize we had unions.

They said, "No. Our union rules say we get this."

"Unions? There are no unions. This is the military!"

So, of course, I learned we did have unions. The union steward came to talk to me about the violations. And yes, the labor agreement did authorize a ten-minute eye-break every hour.

You learn how much you do not know...I had to ask lots of questions to gain an understanding.

So, you learn how much you do not know. You think you know your world, but you learn all these things about loading military and commercial ships. I had never loaded ships before. I had to ask lots of questions to gain an understanding.

In my military advanced course, they glossed over what this military traffic management command did. That was just a fifteen-minute conversation in a training class. But suddenly, I realized all these civilians had to teach me how we load container ships, how we load breakbulk ships, and ammo, and all the different things I needed to know about port operations.

"Did you have people advising you along the way about jobs that would be career-enhancing, and did you typically do some homework and reading to bone up on what you thought you'd need to know before you agreed to take a position?"

Yes and no. I pretty much just took whatever new job that they gave me, but I did call folks who had similar jobs and started learning about that opportunity.

I did have good leaders who pushed me out of my comfort zone—which was a good thing because we all want to stay in our comfort zone. I can remember Colonel Fritz Gruetzmacher saying, "This will be a good opportunity. I want you to take this job."

"I don't have the skill set."

"You're going to learn the skills. You don't walk into any job knowing it."

That was a big click in my brain.

He goes, "You're not supposed to feel comfortable. You take the jobs that make you feel queasy because those are the jobs that you are going to learn more in. If you take the job you know, you're not learning anything."

> **"You're not supposed to feel comfortable. You take the jobs that make you feel queasy because those are the jobs that you are going to learn more in. If you take the job you know, you're not learning anything."**
> **—Colonel Fritz Gruetzmacher**

I commented, "If he had not had that conversation with you, would you have taken that particular job?"

No, I would not have taken that job or even sought it out. I worked for him again later in my career and he continued to push me.

"It sounds like he was one of those instrumental people who made a big difference in your career."

Most certainly.

"Were there other people like him who mentored or pushed you along?"

Yes. There was a battalion commander who gave me career opportunities that I didn't think of. Then, when he would happen to see me later in my career, he would once again say, "Okay, what jobs are you looking at? What are you seeking out?"

Then he would call people and say, "Why don't you consider her for this? I think she can do that."

I didn't realize it, but behind the scenes he was trying to set me up for success by pulling me into jobs that were good.

"You were fortunate to have people looking out for you like that. I would imagine that most people who rise up the ranks have someone in their career who has helped them along."

I think so.

"How long would you typically be in a particular position?"

Normally, you're changing jobs every year. You may stay in the same location for two years, but normally they are putting you in different jobs every year.

They're trying to broaden you. They're trying to give you opportunities to learn more about the military and develop your additional skill sets. As an officer, you are the jack of all trades, the master of none. Whereas your non-commissioned officer and your warrant officer are your experts.

"How important do you think it is to change jobs every year?"

I think it's great. For my junior officers, they always hated it when I moved them. They would say, "I was just beginning to feel comfortable!"

I'd say, "Precisely. That is why you need to go to a new opportunity, where you feel uncomfortable, so you can learn a whole different skill set."

"Do you think that is different in the military than in the corporate world?"

Very different, in some ways. I think you change positions more like every three to five years in the civilian world, not every year. Unless you are in an internship program that is enabling you to move every year, I do not think the corporate world shifts positions as quickly as the military does.

"Do you think this 'do it for a year, master it, and move on' routine is better for the overall organization, or do you find that there are some inefficiencies because people are never perfecting what they do?"

I think you need both. In the military, our non-commissioned officers (NCOs) and warrant officers remain in position longer and become the experts. There may be some inefficiency, but I think it builds effectiveness because the person can look at problems from a totally different perspective. Because they are not encased in the "we've always done it this way" mindset, they can approach solutions differently. They bring in additional knowledge, from other methods of doing things.

Because they are not encased in the "we've always done it this way" mindset, they can approach solutions differently.

It also helps broaden the people they end up working with because they force them to think about other solutions that they might not have ever considered before. So yes, I think it is helpful to an organization to move at least some of the people around, to give them greater breadth and depth.

Now, you cannot have everybody doing that because you need some consistency of people knowing how to get the nuts and bolts done. You need people who know how to make the train schedules work and you need people who can think of how to develop a new train schedule.

"In the corporate world, a common question is, 'If I ultimately want that job over there, what's the typical career path?' From what I am hearing you say, perhaps there are no typical career paths in the military."

I would say that's true.

There are key positions you must accomplish, such as company command, battalion command, brigade command, one-star command. There are command *and* staff jobs that you are expected to have completed. But there is not as much of a cookie-cutter path where only certain jobs will provide you an opportunity to advance.

When you look at my background, it was very diverse. It was not the typical career path that you would have picked for somebody to be deputy commander of USTRANSCOM.

REFLECTIONS:

There is no one "right way" to manage one's career progression. Certainly, taking a widely diverse, cross-functional path to the top is not for everyone, but I can personally attest to how interesting and stimulating it can be for anyone who is curious and loves to learn.

More than half of the women featured in this book credit their cross-functional career path as the key factor that prepared them so well for their ultimate

More than half of the women featured in this book credit their cross-functional career path as the key factor that prepared them so well for their ultimate role at the top.

role at the top. Granted, none of them said that moving into roles for which they had little to no knowledge of or background in was ever easy or without risk.

Some of the downsides of taking a cross-functional approach to managing your career are that you may never feel qualified as you step into each career-broadening position; you may not even know what you do not know, going in. But those things can be resolved by asking lots of questions and being open to learning.

The upsides can be many. Taking a cross-functional career path can give you exposure to so many facets of the business you are in, it can broaden your exposure across your industry and to other cultures, it can enable you to see things from new perspectives, and it can prevent you from getting stuck in a "but we've always done it this way" mindset. It will keep your creative juices flowing.

Best of all, the diversity of skills and knowledge you will acquire along the way can be incredibly powerful. When you finally do reach the top, you *will* be the most qualified candidate to lead the entire organization because you will know more about everything than anyone else.

INTROSPECTIONS:

1. Have you ever volunteered for an assignment that would broaden your expertise? Why or why not? If so, what did you learn?

2. Do you truly love what you do *and* plan to climb the ladder within your functional line of expertise? If so:
   a. What does your ideal career path look like?
   b. Would you consider changing companies or industries to accelerate your advancement? Why or why not?
   c. Would you be willing to take a promotion outside of your current functional area? Why or why not?

3. Based on what you now know, would you be open to pursuing a cross-functional career approach, to broaden your expertise and experience?
   a. If so, what kinds of opportunities might play to your strengths and could provide the environmental factors you would want in the job?
   b. If not, why not? Is it possible that your answer is based on fear, complacency, or a lack of self-confidence—and could you take steps to overcome these blocks?

SEVEN

Fear of Heights

I was turning down the very role I needed to have to make my vision a reality because I did not think I was ready. My father, our board of directors, and a family business consultant helped me realize that it was my vision, my laser focus on an end goal, and my purposeful drive that was needed. At the time, I did not know that. But obviously they were right.

-JODI BERG, PHD
President and CEO, Vita-Mix Corporation

t surprised me to learn that some percentage of high-potential women—at least those who were selected by their senior executives to participate in Business World Rising's Leadership development program—are reluctant to accept promotions to executive-level positions. When I founded my leadership development firm in 2009, I assumed all the women entering our program were readying themselves for that big step to the C-suite—at least those not already there. How wrong I was.

One notable example was a Fortune 500 client—a senior director named Cindy. She was referred to our program by her third-line manager, a female executive vice president.

Cindy was a thirty-two-year-old high-potential who happened to be in the final month of a six-month maternity leave when she was referred into our program. Her EVP thought it might be a nice perk and a gentle way to help this new mom "get her head back into the game" before she officially reentered the workforce.

I asked the EVP what she hoped to accomplish by placing Cindy in our program. She confided that, while Cindy was an extremely bright go-getter, rumor had it she was considering becoming a stay-at-home mom instead of returning to her career. She hoped that by giving Cindy a chance to spend a little grown-up time away from the baby, with other bright and ambitious working mothers, Cindy would come to realize that she could "have it all." The company clearly did not want to lose this rising superstar. In fact, they considered her a strong candidate for senior leadership.

I agreed to enroll Cindy into our program and looked forward to getting to know her. When Cindy finally arrived, we quickly discovered that while she enjoyed the job she had, she was concerned that her immediate manager was out to get her. That was the reason she was considering leaving the firm.

I asked her, "Do you honestly think your executive vice president would enroll you in this leadership development program if your manager was planning to undermine you or fire you?"

She then confided that her boss had suggested that when she returned, she would be placed in a new role in the strategic planning organization to broaden her skills and give her more exposure to the senior executives in other divisions of the company, within and beyond North America. The thought of taking on such a high-visibility role terrified her.

"He knows I don't know anything about global strategy," she told us. "Moving me into a role like that, where I would have to interface with senior executives in other

> **The thought of taking on such a high-visibility role terrified her.**

countries, when I do not even know what they do, would make me look totally inept. I'm pretty sure he has concocted this plan to make me look bad, so I'll quit."

We were stunned that Cindy would even think such a thing. She was obviously a proven high-performer—the kind many large companies slate for executive development. Her misguided belief that her manager was out to get her was an apparent manifestation of her fear of not being ready. How sad it was that Cindy's fear was so overwhelming that she would rather quit than take the chance to shine in such an enviable developmental opportunity.

We responded that just maybe the leaders above her thought she was more capable than anyone else for the role, based on her history of stellar performance before she went on maternity leave.

Cindy was skeptical, but we talked her through alternative ways she could leverage her strengths. To us, this appeared to be the perfect opportunity for her to shine. This was her chance to prove what she really was capable of by tackling it in her own unique way. The fact that she had been selected for our leadership development program in preparation for this new role told us that she was probably on the executive succession plan list. She had never considered that.

Once she returned to work, she shared the challenges of the new role with us. We brainstormed and role-played with her, we gave her feedback on her plans, and hypothesized potential outcomes with her. At the end of each session, she left with an action plan. Each time she returned to meet with us, she reported the outcomes along with her lessons learned. Her confidence level steadily grew.

Within nine months, she was promoted to vice president. Twelve months after that, she was promoted again to become the youngest senior vice president in the company's history.

We All Learn As We Go

Face it, no one knows everything. No CEO steps into the role for the first time knowing precisely how to do the job. Just as discussed in the last chapter about cross-functional experience, the only way to grow your skills, knowledge, and competency is to try new things while leveraging your strengths. You have just got to put yourself out there and step beyond your comfort zone. Executive leadership is just another step along your career path. You learn as you go.

I learned along the way that whenever I tried new things, I always managed to pull it off somehow. The higher visibility the opportunity offered, the more exciting it was to me. The visibility combined with the risk gave me energy. Because of that, I almost always said *yes* to high-risk opportunities, especially if my efforts could potentially have a significant positive impact on the company and our clients.

Of course, to be successful in such endeavors, it is vitally important to know who you are and what you are capable of. You must be able to

> I learned along the way that whenever I tried new things, I always managed to pull it off somehow.

articulate your vision—what you plan to accomplish—along with the story of your personal brand. This applies to anybody, but it is particularly important for women, who in believing they aren't quite ready, are reluctant to step up to the plate, state their intentions, and take a swing at the ball with all they've got—out of fear they will strike out. The reality is, if you don't take that swing, it's impossible to ever hit a home run.

While heading our leadership development program, I came to realize that some women consciously take themselves out of the running for the C-suite succession list. Some women told me they did so because they were afraid that they would have less balance in their lives with a senior-level role.

On the surface, this might seem like a rational concern. Yet, as we paired these self-sidelined mid-level managers with our C-suite members, as part of our peer mentoring program, the mid-levels were surprised to hear what the C-suite women had to share, especially when the mentors asked the mentees, "Do you think you could work any harder than you already do?"

Based on their experience, our senior members shared that leaders do not necessarily work any harder in a C-suite position. One mentor stated, "The reality is that most of us have an imbalance at home—between the woman's role, the man's role, maintaining the home, shopping, cooking, and raising kids. That is the reality. But you are already living and working in that reality and you are already working as hard as you have capacity for anyway."

She went on to say, "There was nothing more going on in the C-suite that could send one over the edge, in terms of work-life balance, unless you simply do not want to be in the boardroom, or the one talking to the investment community, or serve in the role of the company cheerleader."

In general, our C-suite members believed it was possible for a woman to make life better for herself—and for others—by taking on a senior-level role.

I never had a fear of heights, but I understand that some people do, especially women. I find it a shame that without concerted intervention from a coach or a mentor, otherwise bright and talented women too often let unfounded fears derail their upward mobility.

Do not let your fear of heights take you out of the running for executive leadership. There are almost always things you can do to push through

I find it a shame that without concerted intervention from a coach or a mentor, otherwise bright and talented women too often let unfounded fears derail their upward mobility.

your fears, gain new skills, and grow in self-confidence. Before you know it, what once felt impossible will be within your grasp.

I was interested to find out if what we saw in our leadership development program was unique to our program, or if the women on top highlighted in this book saw this same phenomenon—women holding themselves back from jobs at the top.

Melissa Reiff
Former Chairwoman and CEO
The Container Store

I asked Melissa Reiff, "Do you ever see women doing things that make you think, *That is hindering you. That is going to hold you back?*"

Oh, yes, sometimes.

In general, many women do not have enough self-confidence. And they must have humility coupled with it.

For whatever reason, they seem to feel like the mountain is just too hard and too big to climb. They do not feel like they have the support, perhaps, that they need or should have. That makes me sad, and I certainly hope we continue to progress on that front for generations to come.

Everyone is different. Not everyone wants to aspire to a C-suite position and that is *so* okay. We all must be what we want to be. However, no matter what gender or color or whatever, we *all* should have the same equal opportunities. Period.

> **No matter what gender or color or whatever, we *all* should have the same equal opportunities. Period.**

A C-suite role, particularly in a public company, comes with a lot of responsibility. And our board of directors also have a lot of responsibility and a lot of accountability.

> **When you are accountable, you value yourself, and others value you as well. You are appreciated. You matter. Doesn't everybody want to matter?**

I talk a lot in our Coffee Chats to our company about caring—caring, *really* caring—and being 100 percent accountable. That is kind of a cliché, this "I'm going to hold you accountable." But if you really think about it, I cannot believe that there is a human being on the planet who does not want to be accountable. When you are accountable, you value yourself, and others value you as well. You are appreciated. You matter. Doesn't everybody want to matter?

I always say, "Do you think anybody really gets up in the morning and goes, 'Man, I can't wait to have a bad day today'?" I don't think so.

I commented, "I think there can be fear of being held accountable."

There could be fear of being held accountable, for sure. But that also goes back to *how* they are held accountable and who is holding them accountable—how they approach it, the communication, the expectations, and the clarity.

Jodi Berg
President and CEO
Vita-Mix Corporation

Jodi Berg, PhD, shared this insight about her initial lack of enthusiasm when she was offered the chance to become the president of Vitamix:

> I was in the middle of putting various things in place, from a sales and marketing perspective, to transform the company into what we had always wanted it to be, when my father—who, at that point, was the president and CEO—said that he wanted to retire. He asked me if I would step into his position.
>
> I said, "No! Are you crazy? I don't know anything about running a company! I know sales and marketing and   am on to something really big here. I'm going to be a little busy doing that for a while."
>
> So, he talked to the board. He talked to outside consultants and to other people. I finally realized I was the one who had to be convinced.
>
> Originally, I said to him, "I will help you find your replacement. The only thing I ask is that their vision be big enough. It must be as big, or bigger, than mine. I don't want to beat my head against a brick wall, trying to make something happen, when

somebody else is creating a box that is going to hold us back as a company."

I knew a few things.

I knew that we had this incredible opportunity ahead of us. For us to possibly make any of this work, we had to do a total transformation of everything in our company, and we did not have much time.

I was also intimately and personally aware that this was what my great-grandfather wanted when he created a company that focused on making the world a better place around health. This was what my grandparents wanted, and what my parents, my uncles, and my aunts wanted. No pressure, but this was our time!

The third thing I knew was that I was completely unqualified. I knew nothing about being a president or CEO. But I realized that to make my vision happen, to drive the company toward a purpose that I thought was incredibly meaningful, I needed to step up and figure it out.

Fortunately, I also knew that when I focused on a purpose—on an end goal—with a laser focus, I had so much internal drive that I could overcome unbelievable obstacles.

That is when I agreed to become the president and CEO.

If I wanted to make something big happen, instead of being afraid that somebody else would create a box that would hold us back, I needed to make it happen without the limits. I needed to figure out how to make it happen.

I share this, especially when it comes to women.

For whatever reason—either because it is our culture or because it is how we've been raised, men have a significantly higher level of confidence that they can make something happen, even if they don't necessarily have the tools or the experience yet. They have a strong feeling that they can figure it all out.

Instead of being afraid that somebody else would create a box that would hold us back, I needed to make it happen without the limits.

Whereas, for whatever reason—and this is just a general statement—we women tend to say, "Oh, I'm not ready yet. I do not have those skills yet. Somebody else would probably do a better job than I can."

I was turning down the very role I needed to have to make my vision a reality because I did not think I was ready. My father, our board of directors, and a family business consultant helped me realize that it was my vision, my laser focus on an end goal, and my purposeful drive that was needed. At the time, I did not know that. But obviously they were right.

Linda Rutherford
Senior Vice President, Chief Communications Officer
Southwest Airlines

Linda Rutherford shared these insights about moving up to the executive suite:

Every time you take on a role, I think one of the things that women struggle with is that we straddle the roles sometimes. We get stuck in what is comfortable about doing the *old* job. We do not fully transition into the *new* job.

I read a book by David Cottrell called *Monday Morning Leadership.* That was an inspiration for me. He called it "the difference between being a driver and a passenger."

He wrote, "You've got to allow yourself the time to understand that those roles are different, and you have to consciously say what you're going to do differently to create new habits." That was an eye-opener for me. It was very helpful.

> **Moving away from the day-to-day operations and more into the corporate strategy, being a peer adviser to officers who are in the executive suite, is just a different role.**

Moving away from the day-to-day operations and more into the corporate strategy, being a peer adviser to officers who are in the executive suite, is just a different role. I had to give myself time to transition and I had to be intentional about it.

I asked Linda, "Did you initially feel intimidated by having the word *chief* in your title?"

I will be honest. There is a managing director of communication and outreach who is an officer of the company. There is a managing director of culture and engagement who is an officer of the company. They both report to me. They are responsible for the day-to-day operation of their functions.

I think the only thing I worried about, in terms of being the "chief" is that I knew that meant the executives in the C-suite would still come ask me questions. I needed to create space for those two leaders to have their own opportunity to lead. They both happen to be women, and they need their opportunity to lead.

My concern about "chief" was that it would overshadow their opportunity to be able to show their talents and capabilities. So, again, being very intentional, I need to make sure that each of those leaders has an opportunity to be seen by the board of directors, to be involved in debates and conversations about knotty topics related to communication, culture, or employee engagement, so that my peers can see them as capable, strong leaders who are up for the challenge, too.

I responded, "Can we assume that your former boss, Ginger, did that for you, as well?"

She absolutely did. I learned that from her.

"So, you knew what it felt like to have that exposure—or to not have that exposure. She set you up."

Right. You are absolutely right.

"Was it a surprise for you when Ginger left?"

Oh, yes. It was a shock. I remember when she called me into her office. I thought she was going to tell me about some assignment I was getting. When she told me she was retiring, I burst into tears.

But she said, "It's time. I have done what I can do here. I'm so happy and blessed. I have you, who can totally step into the role. You are ready."

Anyway, it was a shock. I really thought there would be two or three more years in there, so it was a big surprise.

Then, of course, everything was just crazy. Literally a month later, Teresa Laraba, our senior vice president of customers—whom you interviewed in your previous books—passed away. There was a lot of upheaval with me being new in the role, Ginger's retiring, and Teresa's passing away. There was a lot going on there.

REFLECTIONS:

Not everyone aspires to be in the C-suite, nor should they, considering there are only so many C-suite positions. However, women who are capable and deemed by higher-ups to be high-potential candidates should never take themselves out of the running due to unfounded fears.

- If you have already taken yourself out of the running for a top-level role, reconsider your reasoning.
- If you believe you would have more work-life *imbalance* at the top, consider that you could potentially make life better for yourself—and for others—if you were in the top position.
- If you think you would not like the kind of work that senior executives are responsible for, consider that you could

delegate those activities you do not like to do or do not excel in. Granted, not all activities can be delegated, but many can.

- If you simply do not know enough about what goes on at the top, seek out stretch assignments or promotional opportunities that give you the opportunity to interact with senior leaders. Doing so may not only broaden your experience, but it could also give you more self-confidence.
- If you are afraid of public speaking or interacting with the media, join Toastmasters or start accepting local speaking engagements, starting now. If you feel you need speaking or media coaching, get it. There are a variety of resources out there to help with that.

Bottom line: Do not let a fear of the unknown hold you back. At the very least, request informational interviews

Do not let a fear of the unknown hold you back.

with senior executives to learn more about what they do. Start with those who lead functional areas that interest you. Of course, be mindful and respectful of their time, and be well prepared with questions going in, but at least make the effort to learn more about what those roles entail. What you learn might surprise you, and you might get some great exposure at the same time.

INTROSPECTIONS:

1   Do you really know what it is like to be in the C-suite? If not, do you know anyone who is there, or who has been there, whom you could speak to about their experience?

2   Have you "quit before you even got started," meaning, have you deliberately taken yourself off the track to the C-suite? If so, why?

3   If you have ever turned down a skills-broadening or high-visibility opportunity, why did you do that? Knowing what you know now, what could you have done differently?

4   Remember, it is never too late. How might you reposition yourself for advancement, starting now?

EIGHT

Impostor Syndrome

*I have certainly felt like I was not really as authentic
as others are as the woman on top.*
- WENDY JOHNSON
Former President and CEO, Dale Carnegie franchise, Atlanta, GA

M ost everyone feels self-doubt from time to time. It's a
normal human condition and has a purpose. After all,
being overly confident can get us into trouble if we fail to
recognize potential threats and dangers. Steadfastly believing we
can conquer everything and anything at all costs can have serious
consequences in certain cases. In extreme cases, feelings of
uncertainty can actually save our lives.

Yet those same feelings can cause us to hold ourselves back, even
when we already have everything that we need to step forward, to
serve as an inspirational role model, and lead the way.

You might be surprised to know that even some of the most successful business executives and military leaders suffer from self-doubt occasionally. Some executives have lived out their careers feeling like fakes, even while appearing to lead highly successful lives. This kind of nagging self-doubt in those who have already risen to the top is referred to as *the impostor syndrome.*

Edward E. Whitacre, Jr., both a former chairman and CEO of General Motors Company and a retired chairman and CEO of AT&T, talked about his own dealings with the impostor syndrome in the foreword he wrote to the book by Joyce M. Roché, *The Empress Has No Clothes: Conquering Self-Doubt to Embrace Success* (Berrett-Koehler Publishers, Inc.). In his words, "There's this nagging doubt in the back of your mind that says, 'Maybe I don't know this as well as somebody else. Maybe I'm just a fake.'"

What finally got him over the hump of the impostor syndrome was something his second-line manager—his boss's boss—once said to him: "You have to be out with your people instead of sitting in the office."

As Whitacre wrote in his foreword, "I never forgot that lesson and have, throughout my career, made it my highest priority to get to know the people I work with. And what I discovered was that it helped me deal with my own self-doubts, especially as I advanced and eventually became a CEO; I wanted a company that was sort of a family."

Whitacre went on to explain, "No matter what, I always had the confidence in my ability to get along with other people. And I guess after a time, I learned to get along with myself as well. It's not that I didn't feel uncertain of myself or even like an impostor in new situations; it just took less time to find my balance and to give myself credit."

Great advice.

I struggled with self-doubt early in my career as a systems engineer, both at AT&T and at IBM, while working in male-dominated environments where many of the men I worked with, both internally and my clients, were extremely technical and far senior to me in terms in tenure in the business. Early on, I assumed they knew way more than I did. That scared me, but it also caused me to really dig in and do my homework.

Early on, I assumed they knew way more than I did. That scared me, but it also caused me to really dig in and do my homework.

As a result, I learned to ask a lot of questions, rather than simply spew forth what little I knew, especially when I was around men who seemed to know their stuff *and* who were willing to mentor me. Eventually, I grew comfortable admitting when I did not have an immediate answer. I would commit to learning more about whatever questions these clients had. In turn, they were impressed when I did my homework and then got back to them with verified details and explanations.

Pretty soon, anticipating their questions and doing my homework in advance of such meetings gave me the confidence to just be myself. I eventually learned I could build more trusting relationships by simply admitting when I was unsure about something. It always seemed to serve me well to say, "I don't know. Tell me what you know, and I'll get back to you with more information ASAP."

Better yet, doing my homework gave me the confidence to speak up if I believed I knew some aspect of an issue better than they did, or

Having just a little self-doubt along with some humility can be a good thing.

when I had a suggestion or a differing opinion. I also learned that having a little bit of self-doubt kept me from coming off as a know-it-all. Having just a little self-doubt along with some humility can be a good thing.

Don't Let Self-Doubt Hold You Back

Some people let self-doubt get in the way of their advancement when it really should not. I will highlight one such example here.

A female executive friend of mine, by most any measure, has had a highly successful career. She is well liked by most everyone who knows her, and she has long held a reputation for being an ambitious go-getter. I was stunned when she confided in me about her own struggles with the impostor syndrome.

Much like me, for several years she reported to a female boss whom she greatly admired, respected, and enjoyed working for.

She was thrilled to follow in her boss's footsteps, in job after job, as her female boss rose through the ranks to the executive suite. What I had never realized before, though, was that my friend suffered from recurring bouts of self-doubt all the while.

She finally shared this story with me one day:

> I must be honest with you. While I learned what I needed to learn about leadership from her, I did not think I could do her job each time she was promoted because I believed she was perfect. I truly thought that her way was the only way that anyone could possibly be as successful as she was in that role.
>
> I observed the relationships that she had with the people who are now my peers. I always thought to myself, *I'm not wired that way. I could never approach problem-solving the way she does.*
>
> I know everybody is different and I am totally fine with that. But I told myself, *There is no way I can follow in her footsteps and perform as well as she has done.*
>
> When she eventually left the company, she said to me, "You are ready to step into this role now. I've told the CEO I am recommending you as my replacement. All you need to do is ask him for it, and my job will be yours."
>
> I was scared to death! I honestly thought there was no way I could do her job. And yes, I had that feeling every single time I backfilled her in each of her former roles. I had observed how she did things for so long, with her own unique style and

grace, I was completely convinced there was simply no way I could ever do anything as well as she did.

Thankfully, every time she was promoted, and I had the chance to backfill her previous slot, I always decided I would just have to get over it and do things my own way. While I was sure I would never be as good as she was, I was able to convince myself that I would at least be okay at it. Someone was going to get the job, so why not me? Turns out, I have always been more than just okay.

Now that I'm where I am today, I've had the chance to have great conversations with our CEO and other leaders in our C-suite. Virtually all of them have said to me, "We're so glad you decided to accept this role and make it your own, and that you didn't feel like you had to pattern yourself after someone else. Here are all the things we loved about your predecessor, but here are the things we really love about you...."

> **Someone was going to get the job, so why not me? Turns out, I have always been more than just okay.**

That's been very affirming. If only I had known that sooner, I could have spared myself a lot of anxiety.

My friend's experience is not unusual, and it is a key lesson for women to grasp.

Based on my own interactions with our leadership development clients, I know many women feel intimidated when they are offered the chance to follow in the footsteps of another woman who has been a highly admired role model. Consequently, some will either shun promotional opportunities, or will push themselves to follow in their predecessor's footsteps while considering themselves as "fake" due to their inept attempts to emulate their predecessor's strengths rather than leveraging their own gifts and talents. They fail to believe that doing things in their own unique way might be even better than the way their role model did things.

Having personally mentored many women leaders at all levels on the career ladder, I **The biggest challenge many otherwise highly capable women have is their own self-talk.** can attest that the biggest challenge many otherwise highly capable women have is their own self-talk—all those negative warning messages that play inside their heads.

I have heard plenty of women, and even some men, admit to saying to themselves such things as, *Oh, my gosh. Oh, my gosh. Can you really handle this? You have really taken on a big one this time. Woah! You better rethink this.*

It is true that the element of being uncomfortable or worried— because you are moving into a new area and you may not know what you are talking about—can be healthy. It can keep you from being too cocky and it can prevent you from taking risky actions you really cannot handle. On the other hand, the energy it takes to manage overly critical self-talk can be draining. That energy could be far better spent.

Most casual observers might not ever believe that otherwise polished, self-confident, and successful individuals could possibly suffer from such negative talk. Some might even believe such highly capable individuals are egotistical, which is the outward manifestation of impostor syndrome.

> **Some might even believe such highly capable individuals are egotistical, which is the outward manifestation of impostor syndrome.**

Each of us may be familiar with senior leaders who seem to have an overbalance of confidence versus humility. As Melissa Reiff said, great leaders have a good balance of humility and confidence.

We coached our leadership development clients to ask themselves two questions whenever they started hearing that negative self-talk:

1. "When have you ever failed?"
2. "What in your history makes you think you are going to fail this time?"

Once these women admitted to themselves that they had never failed before—or if they had, they learned much from the experience and were able to get right back in the saddle without injury—they were then better able to move forward.

If only more women could have the self-confidence to be proud of who they are, especially when someone has recommended them for promotion. Just imagine how much more impactful we could

all be if we could overcome the impostor syndrome and become
all that we are destined to be.

The women interviewed in this book are such amazing role models
that I could not have imagined any of them would have ever
struggled with the impostor syndrome. Yet, as you'll see, they all
knew exactly what I was talking about, and many of them
admitted to having these feelings themselves and/or seeing them
in other women.

Jodi Berg
President and CEO
Vita-Mix Corporation

It was interesting how Jodi Berg, PhD, responded when I posited,
"What have you noticed women doing, whether at the Ritz-
Carlton, or at Vitamix, or elsewhere in your journeys across the
world, that might hinder their advancement?" While she did not
use the term *impostor syndrome*, she essentially described it.

> One of the things I see is that we don't believe that we can
> figure it out.
>
> We're hesitant to take something on unless we feel like we
> already have a solution or something that we can apply to it.
> This happens to be more of a tendency in women. It does not
> mean there aren't men out there who struggle with exactly

this same thing. And it does not at all mean that all women struggle with it.

But if you do struggle with that—and I have met so many people who have—find your network of people who already have ideas or resources that can help you through it, so when you are faced with a situation that you do not have an answer for, you can quickly figure it out.

It's not just about promotions and moving up. It is about any obstacle that you face. The thing that I think is so fascinating is that there is no training manual on how to be a mom. There are lots of books written on the subject, but how many of us read through all those books before we become a mom? Then, once you become a mom, you are so busy that you cannot take the time to read them.

Regarding being a mom, I have two daughters. But in both cases, they are so incredibly different from each other that everything I thought I had down to a science from raising one child,

Everything that we come across, we must figure it out—and we do!

I might as well have thrown out the window because the second child was so different. So, everything that we come across, we must figure it out—and we do!

But then you put us in the work world, and we are thinking, *Okay. There must be some way to do this that somebody else knows. Certainly, I do not know, and I am not sure that I can figure it out.*

The fact is, we have this, gals! It is in us! We do it all the time! But for some reason, we turn it into a limitation when we get into the work world.

I responded, "That's a great analogy: 'There is no manual for being a parent.' Maybe you had great role model parents; maybe you did not. But the most important thing on the planet that we do is raise happy, successful people."

Well, we can say *relatively* happy and successful people. Don't set the bar too high. We have to be realistic.

"Well, we have to figure out how to raise these children."

And we do! We figure it out. We figure out incredibly complicated things that nobody else has experienced before, at least in our world, that we're aware of. We figure it out.

Yet we don't have the same confidence in the work environment. That would be, probably, the biggest thing that I see holding women back.

The other thing that I see that holds women back is this feeling that they will be more successful if they do something the same way that somebody else has done it, versus truly believing in themselves.

I think the belief that we must follow in somebody else's footsteps—versus realizing that maybe we have something special that we uniquely bring to the table, something that somebody else would not necessarily have—that would be the other thing that I think holds us back.

Nancy Howell Agee
President and CEO
Carilion Clinic

Nancy Agee, president and CEO of Carilion Clinic, and I discussed the impostor syndrome. I asked her, "Why is it that some women make excuses for themselves, as though they don't believe they are as good as they think they should be?"

Yes, you do not hear that as commonly from men.

"It seems somewhat common for women to decline going after an opportunity if they don't believe they meet 100 percent of the criteria for the job."

Yep. I agree.

"Yet, a man who meets just 30 percent of the criteria will go, 'Hey! I've got 30 percent of these. I can do this.'"

Yes, and they'll often get the job.

"When I was running my leadership development organization, I would raise this issue with female CEOs, or women just under the CEO. It was quite an eye-opener. I would say, 'Think about it. When you are the hiring manager, or you are the chairman of the board selecting someone for the CEO position, who are you going to put in there? Are you going to pick the one who says, *Well, I'm not sure,* regardless of their background, or the one who says, *I can do this. Put me in there?*'"

I do not know why we do this. You've probably read a lot about the impostor

> **When you are the hiring manager...are you going to pick the one who says, *Well, I'm not sure*, regardless of their background, or the one who says, *I can do this. Put me in there*?**

syndrome. Almost all the studies about the impostor syndrome have been about women.

I think it was a woman, P.R. Clance, who first did the study. Her thesis, *The Impostor Phenomenon*, found it was more common in women. But certainly, it can apply to both men and women.

Linda Rutherford
Senior Vice President, Chief Communications Officer
Southwest Airlines

Linda Rutherford, Southwest Airlines' chief communications officer, answered in a similar way when I asked her, "What are some of the things that you observe women do that hinders their advancement?"

I think sometimes we mute ourselves. We should not do that. I think sometimes we let that little negative

> **Sometimes we let that little negative self-talker in the back of our brain rule the day.**

self-talker in the back of our brain rule the day.

I think we worry too much about saying something that would convince people that we are not ready for the job, which is a cousin to muting yourself. We have a perspective, but then we will not share it.

For example, even though I'm talkative and I have a strong voice, I was having a mental block when I was in the VP role and we would be in the boardroom. That's where the top executives go in and the subjects change. Every time I went in that room, I turned into a mute person. I couldn't speak above a whisper. I would just get completely drenched in sweat.

I had to train myself. It probably took about eighteen months, but now I don't have that physical reaction anymore. Now I know that these people are my friends and we're just going to have a conversation.

I think those are the biggest things that we do that hinder ourselves.

Wendy Johnson
Former President and CEO
Dale Carnegie franchise, Atlanta, GA

When I spoke with Wendy Johnson, former president and CEO of Dale Carnegie of Georgia, she also brought up the impostor syndrome.

I do not know if you have ever talked to women who say, "I am afraid I'll be found out that I'm an empty suit."

I think because I worked for smaller organizations for years, and I did not go through formal management training, I have certainly felt like I was not really as authentic as others are as the woman on top.

I know so many female executives who were identified as high-potentials, so they went through a leadership development process within their organizations. Their companies developed them. They had the ability to move from one functional area to another, based on the development plan created for them.

I envied that. I felt that they were much more authentic as leaders than I was.

When you have the kind of checkerboard career that I had, it can create a lack of self-confidence. Well, not confidence so much, but you do wonder if you are an impostor.

When you have the kind of checkerboard career that I had...you do wonder if you are an impostor.

I replied, "Yes, it's kind of like, 'Do I really want to be here when there are people who are probably more qualified?'"

Right. And they have more education, too. They'll even have MBAs and other certifications, which I think is fabulous.

But looking back on all that now, in actuality, I was quite agile and passionate because of the way my career played out.

Lieutenant General Kathleen M. Gainey
U.S. Army, Retired

As I did with each of the other women highlighted in this book, I asked Lt. Gen. Kathy Gainey, "What type of things do you see women do, whether they're in the military or civilians, that might hinder their advancement?"

I think sometimes we try too hard.

I started out trying too hard early on. I was trying to just be one of the guys instead of being myself. I did not wear makeup. I cut my hair very, very short. I started cussing.

I thought I had to act like a guy to be successful.

That was not me. But I was trying to be successful. I thought I had to act like a guy to be successful. What I realized was, 1) I did not like that, 2) it was not effective, and 3) why did I think I had to?

So, my dad helped me with that. He asked me, "Why do you think you have to be like them?"

"Well, I have got to be like the guys if I'm going to fit in and succeed."

"I don't think so, and I'm in the military."

"But you're a guy!"

"Well, just try the other way a little."

So, I realized that I could be myself.

I commented, "It seems there's a reluctance for some leaders to admit, 'I don't know.' Was there a point in your career when you felt comfortable enough to admit that you didn't know everything, and ask people who were junior to you to teach you or show you the ropes?"

> I had a very good platoon sergeant who coached and mentored me from day one. Not knowing my background, not knowing I had a father in the military, he just showed up on day one and said, "Lieutenant, happy to have you on board in our platoon. Get settled in. I'll be back at 6:00 p.m. Here are your coveralls. Have them on." And he walked away.

> At 6:00 he came back and said, "Okay, Lieutenant. We're going to the motor pool. I'm going to teach you how to do a service [maintenance] on this piece of equipment, because tomorrow the platoon is going to be doing that and you're going to need to inspect them. You're going to need to know how to inspect, so I'm going to teach you tonight."

> So, for three hours he showed me how the vehicle was going to be broken down, all the maintenance that needed to be done, and how to check to see if they were doing it correctly. He did that for every event, even before we went to the field for training.

> He said, "Okay. We are going to set up this tent out here behind our building. You're going to dig the trench. You're going to learn which poles go where. You're going to see how to check the tautness of the rope, to make sure that this

doesn't fall apart in the rain and that it doesn't get wet because you didn't tie it down correctly."

He would teach me all those things so that when we went out to conduct the training, I knew how to check. They simply can't teach you everything in that initial three-month military school, before you go to your first unit.

I replied, "How wonderful that you had someone who was willing to do that for you. Was that the platoon sergeant's job?"

That is their job. A platoon sergeant's job is to teach their young officer, their NCOs (non-commissioned officers), and the soldiers.

Now, a young officer must be humble enough to admit that they don't know everything. We are taught that, but it is another thing if you did not accept that your subordinate would be teaching you.

Officers sometimes think that they are better than their NCO. More educated? More than likely, yes. But that NCO is going to have had at least five to seven years' more experience than you, and the soldiers have at least two to three years' more experience than you. So, you can learn from every level.

REFLECTIONS:

If you believe you suffer from impostor syndrome, no matter what step of the career ladder you are currently on, now is the time to acknowledge it and do what it takes to address it. The good news is, as you have seen in this chapter, there are several practical tools that can help you overcome impostor syndrome.

- Do not turn down a promotional opportunity to follow in your manager's footsteps if that manager has recommended you to backfill their position. If they tell you that you are ready for the role, then believe them and believe in your own unique style and abilities. You do not have to do it like anyone else. Make the job your own.

- If you hear yourself saying, "I don't think I can do this," remind yourself of all the fantastic things you have

  There is always a first time for everything. Have confidence that you will figure out what to do this time, too.

  done. There is always a first time for everything. Have confidence that you will figure out what to do this time, too.

- A little bit of worry can be healthy. It will keep you striving to do your best.

- If those self-doubt voices continue to play inside your head, be your own coach and tell yourself to "Just stop it!" and listen to something you love, like great music or an inspirational audio book.

- Be humble enough to admit what you do not know and always be willing to learn.

- If you need extra help, seek it out. There are plenty of people who can assist you, from professional coaches and people in your own network, to training classes, peer mentoring programs, and more. Do not be afraid to ask for help when you need it. Your company might even pay for it.

- Remember, it takes practice to develop good self-help skills. Keep practicing and eventually you will master it.

INTROSPECTIONS:

1   Has your own self-doubt ever precluded you from moving forward in your career? If so, based on what you now know, what issues might you be able to overcome going forward?

2   Have you ever turned down a career opportunity because you thought you would not do it as well as the previous person in that position? If so, make a list of the unique skills you could have brought to the table. What is it about your personal style that could have allowed you to shine?

3   What special tips have you now learned that you could share with other women to help them quiet their own negative self-talk?

4   What changes can you make or actions can you take to increase your knowledge/skills so you can stop feeling like an impostor?

NINE

Leading Through Influence

Your role, in the senior levels, is about developing relationships and nurturing relationships with other organizations, and within your own organization. It is both internal and external. So, when you need to make things happen, you have already spoken with these people before. You've had coffee. You've shared philosophies.

When you need to start developing a solution with people you have never met before, it is hard to get in the door. If you have already established a relationship, they will at least return your phone call.

-LT. GEN. KATHLEEN M. GAINEY
U.S. Army, Retired

L eadership through influence is all about shaping the hearts and minds of great numbers of people who are not necessarily within your direct span of control. For some, this can be the most difficult leadership skill to master, yet it is the most valuable.

One of the greatest gifts I received early in my career was the education that came along with working in a Fortune 100 sales organization, selling to government accounts and other major corporations, and developing relationships with our global technology partners. Not only did I learn to lead my own team (however small or large it might be), I learned to lead my peers, my managers, my clients, and our business partners *through influence*. This lesson has paid dividends throughout my life.

In my opinion, one of the best things about being in sales—aside from the nice commissions one can earn—or being in a sales-supporting role, is the tremendous opportunity to learn to lead through influence. When you are paid to close and deliver on big-ticket sales deals, it is essential to build warm, caring, and trusting relationships with individuals at all levels and across many functional areas. You have to do this if you are to have a prayer of making your numbers.

In sales, one learns quickly that people buy from those they like and trust. You either learn that right away or you kiss your commissions goodbye. These skills will serve you well in every aspect of your life, for the rest of your life, regardless of where you go or what you do, and most especially in leadership.

If you read my first book, *The WOW Factor Workplace: How to Create a Best Place to Work Culture*, you may recall the story of how I was thrust into my first sales position. When the salesman I supported at AT&T up and quit one day, his sales manager, Betty, offered me his job. I accepted the position only once she convinced me that the main reason our clients bought from us was due to the trusting and influential relationships I had established within our accounts.

I had never seen myself as all that influential, but apparently I was. Betty convinced me that I simply needed to continue doing what I had been doing to be successful in sales. She was right. Believe it or not, being successful in business-to-business sales is the epitome of leading through influence.

The most effective and beloved leaders pretty much do the same thing. They strive to understand what their team members, their peers, the overall organization, their business partners, shareholders, and clients need. They create and deliver solutions that solve their problems and meet their objectives. They also do their best to achieve what I call "Infinite-Win" outcomes—meaning outcomes that not only benefit those individuals, but the broader community as well.

> **The most effective and beloved leaders...strive to understand what their team members, their peers, the overall organization, their business partners, shareholders, and clients need.**

Winning Hearts and Minds

I had the chance to really up my leading through influence game, beyond a sales role, when I was promoted to run the AT&T Information Systems southwest regional executive conference center. In addition to managing the team that hosted important client executive briefings, it was my responsibility to coordinate executive golf tournaments and other executive events for the purpose of forging relationships between our own executives and those of our largest accounts.

By establishing close, trusting relationships between the companies' top brass, it was far easier for our sales teams to win the big deals. Commitments could essentially be made at the executive level on a handshake. It was interesting to learn how this worked.

Soon after, IBM recruited me to help establish influential relationships between certain IBM product development executives and those of AT&T's biggest competitors. It was an IBM strategic objective to capture the burgeoning voice/data integration market through joint product development ventures with these new technology partners. This business development role enabled me to take my leading through influence skills to a whole new level. A few years later, IBM made the big shift away from providing consulting and support services free of charge, as part of the sale of a mainframe computer, to selling computers and fee-based professional services separately.

After that big change, professional services staff members— consultants, project managers, applications developers, etc.—all reported to a manager who was simply responsible for overseeing the staff's billable hours, timecard reporting, and performance reviews. The professional services staff members could pick and choose the billable projects they worked on.

Meanwhile, a new professional services manager role was created, of which I was one. As such, I was responsible for the sale and delivery of certain fee-based services to clients, but I had no direct staff management responsibility. Instead, I had to win the hearts and minds of the very best, most talented professional services delivery personnel. I essentially had to entice them to work on the service engagements I was responsible to deliver.

Net-net, as part of this big organizational restructure, IBM put matrix management in place. Matrix management is an organizational structure by which individuals report to two managers. Professional services team members maintained a solid-line relationship to their personnel manager, while they had a temporary, dotted-line relationship to me for the duration of my project.

Some people loathe matrix management structures. As the subordinate, one has to deal with two managers who don't necessarily have complementary objectives; as the project leader, one must get things done by winning hearts and minds. Successful matrix management is essentially dependent upon enabling people to do what they do best and love to do. I happen to be a big fan, at least in terms of managing ad hoc or otherwise short-term projects. If you do it right, it can be incredibly fulfilling for one and all—a true Infinite-Win.

Bottom line: Successful business-to-business sales, leading successful projects, and a whole host of other outcomes are highly dependent upon one's ability to build and maintain strong, trusting, and enriching relationships, both within and beyond your organization, with people who do not directly report to you. If your objective is to lead at the C-suite level, you must be effective at leading through influence.

Face it, leading through influence—building and maintaining solid, trusting relationships with people beyond your direct span of control—is key to one's success in life. Yet, some people never seem to figure this out.

Leading through influence—building and maintaining solid, trusting relationships with people beyond your direct span of control—is key to one's success in life.

Those who fail to get their arms around the basic tenets of Dale Carnegie's long-revered book, *How to Win Friends and Influence People,* are not likely to make it to the C-suite.

Wendy Johnson
Former President and CEO
Dale Carnegie franchise, Atlanta, GA

Wendy Johnson shared two stories about leading through influence—one about some of her Dale Carnegie clients, and another about how she led through influence as a flight attendant.

> I think many young people entering the workforce have little or poor communication and relationship-building skills. Their English is truncated. They use acronyms for everything. They do not know how to write a business letter. They do not communicate when they really need to. The reason they do not know how is because a great deal of what they have learned to do has been on a screen.

I asked, "Did you find that to be a growing trend based on the folks attending the Dale Carnegie program?"

Yes. Their bosses were sending them because they needed to learn communication and relationship skills.

I will describe a scenario that we saw happening in the hiring process:
- A candidate would go through the company's interview process.
- They would get the offer.
- They would accept the offer.
- Then they would not even show up for their first day of work.

It is called *ghosting.* It is common. Clearly, this person did not possess the basic communication skills and did not understand the importance of relationship ethics.

It is also common for a millennial—the younger ones, not the older ones—to come to work for you, but then they just stop coming to work. They would not even call their manager or anyone else to let them know that they were not coming back. That is also what they call *ghosting.*

I commented, "It sounds like they just quit, but they don't bother to tell anyone they quit."

Right.

Then you have the situation where a company manager is conducting a job interview, and the parents of the interviewee want to talk to the company manager! That is the absolute ultimate.

"As a hiring manager, a parent's intervention would cause me to think, *No. I do not care who this person is. We are not hiring them.*"

There are many examples of how differently our newer generations behave. Some have formed workstyles that reflect their parents' own negative experiences in the corporate world—such as from downsizings and layoffs—and based on their own exposure to the digital world.

Those whose parents worked late and had great work ethics are, themselves, likely to work late and have great work ethics. But others, depending on how they were brought up, are subscribers to "work-life balance" principles. For example, even though they know that a big proposal is due by midnight tonight, at five o'clock they will say, "See you later," and they will leave for the day, with the proposal left for others to finish.

Some millennials, though certainly not all, are unreliable from the standpoint of putting in the extra effort. They are fickle, not loyal to the corporation. They might be loyal to their team, or to the product, but not to the company. They believe in work-life balance, but they have taken the concept to a whole new level. They act more like free agents.

So, there are a lot of relationship challenges. And if you can't build strong relationships, you can't be an influential leader. In fact, you won't get ahead or even get started on the first step of the ladder if you don't show up for others.

If you can't build strong relationships, you can't be an influential leader.

I think this current generation that is now coming out of college is even more tied to their screens. In some cases, screens have taken over their lives. Maybe the training needs to change to accommodate that, but I still believe that it is hard to build trust from a screen. Trust is the basis of good business relationships.

I do not think *in-person* training will ever totally go away. Yet, sadly, I believe the ability to demonstrate good skills for *in-person* communication is decreasing because people are not getting the practice they need. Practicing in-person communication is more effective than screen practice.

Now that they are going to college online, what is this going to look like?

I shared my own perspective. "Yes, it is scary from a corporate standpoint. But on the other hand, those who do develop strong relationship-building skills are really going to stand out and shine like superstars."

Yes, I agree.

I cannot tell you how many times we had people in our program who nobody wanted to work with. Some were about to be fired because others did not want them directing anything or anyone—they would be too harsh to those around them.

In our training, they learned that it is okay to be nice, but firm. In fact, that was more effective. They learned that bringing people around to their point of view gently is more effective than shouting orders. Our training would take the sharp edges off people.

Some people talk too loudly and are boisterous. Senior leaders do not want to promote those people into client-facing roles because they cannot count on them to keep the volume at a level for the interaction to be successful. We would have those participants whisper their class presentations to learn more about the possible ranges of their voices.

Bringing people around to [your] point of view gently is more effective than shouting orders.

Because our programs use public speaking as the medium to effect change, we can work on such habits in real time. Everyone speaks multiple times during each session. It is amazing to watch the magic happening. We coach them by saying, "Lower, lower. No, I mean lower," until they finally become aware of their range of volume. There is not just one range—which, for them, was loud.

For the ones who would speak too softly, we would do the opposite. We would make them scream. I mean *scream*. They were never really the same after that because once you allow yourself to step outside of your self-imposed boundaries, you have a new imprint, with new muscle memory that you can draw from. Those people soared professionally once their communication skills were improved.

Wendy then went on to tell a story that demonstrates how anyone, whether they're an "official" authority figure or not, can lead through influence. If you are willing to pay attention to what's going on around you and have the courage to speak up when you see something that isn't working, you'll be valued and appreciated. And you can play a pivotal role in making improvements to your organization.

Years ago, when I was working for Pan Am as a flight attendant, I used to see things that I thought the

If you are willing to pay attention to what's going on around you and have the courage to speak up when you see something that isn't working, you'll be valued and appreciated.

airline needed to do to improve. So I would write letters. One time I wrote a letter to Pan Am management about a marketing program they had implemented on their Puerto Rican route.

At the time, Pan Am was competing with American Airlines. Back then, American Airlines flights to Puerto Rico had a very popular singles-type bar at the back of their planes. Their passengers would go to this bar and socialize during their journey. This bar was getting a lot of press, and t increased their business.

So, Pan Am was trying to compete, but they could not compete very well, because they did not own the kind of aircraft that allowed for a bar in the back of the plane. Instead, Pan Am hired mariachi bands to stroll through the plane. Mariachis! It was completely out of control.

I mean, we flight attendants could not even get our carts down the aisles because we had these mariachis in the way. We were serving hamburgers and hot dogs, and we provided dominos instead of playing cards.

So, I wrote a letter to some of the Pan Am managers and shared my observations. "This marketing project is not resonating with anyone and it's actually awful in terms of service excellence."

They contacted me and arranged for me to have an interview with J. Walter Thompson, the advertising company. I went to meet with them in Puerto Rico. It was awesome. They eventually ended that promotion.

Then, another time, I went to a Pan Am town hall meeting where I was offering my opinions on various promotions. I offered to do other work for them during my time off. Getting their attention, they placed me in a management training program. I was in my early twenties at the time.

They flew me to Pan Am headquarters in New York. That was back when we were in the Pan Am building in New York City. They had me interview with every single vice president in the company. I could ask them questions and talk about their experiences. The objective was for me to pick an area that I would be interested in pursuing for a new role with Pan Am. It was really fascinating to me.

One executive I interviewed was the vice president of catering. Pan Am had just recently implemented a huge, worldwide cuisine change, and I was wondering about it. I asked this executive, "I would just love to know your history with the company. Why did you change the cuisine?"

He responded, "I'm so glad you asked that question. When I joined the airline, the first thing I did was get on a Pan Am airplane. I would fly all over the world, undercover. Whenever I landed in a city, I would go straight to catering to find the dishwashers. I would roll up my sleeves and wash dishes with them. This gave me the opportunity to ask them questions."

"Really? What would you ask them?"

"What are you throwing out? What aren't people eating?"

He discovered valuable information about the international menus. They were completely ridiculous—there was so much waste. They were flying strawberries in the belly of the plane, from one city to another just so they could serve strawberries when there were no strawberries in the local town.

So, he changed to a menu where they could utilize the fresh food available from the local country. They would feature native foods from that local country, rather than try to be highfalutin, flying to India but serving French food.

I never forgot this wisdom. When he started his job, the first thing he did was roll up his sleeves and go right to the most knowledgeable source of information and ask questions. He uncovered the facts so he could make effective decisions. He believed in understanding the

When he started his job, the first thing he did was roll up his sleeves and go right to the most knowledgeable source of information and ask questions.

whole transaction, from end to end. I never, ever forgot that.

I ended up choosing recruiting and was promoted into that role. I used the wisdom I learned from this catering VP throughout my career, but what got me there was my interest in the excellence of my company and then speaking up.

Lieutenant General Kathleen M. Gainey
U.S. Army, Retired

Lt. Gen. Kathy Gainey shared this insight about leading through influence:

> Something people do not necessarily realize about senior leadership is that it is all about networking and relationships.
>
> Your role, in the senior levels, is about developing relationships and nurturing relationships with other organizations, and within your own organization. It is both internal and external. So, when you need to make things happen, you have already spoken with these people before. You've had coffee. You've shared philosophies.
>
> When you need to start developing a solution with people you have never met before, it is hard to get in the door. If you have already established a relationship, they will at least return your phone call.

I asked her, "How much of the senior officer or general officer role is dealing with people outside the military?"

> It's a significant amount, particularly as you go up higher in rank. You are dealing more with civilians who are in other governmental organizations and in civilian companies.
>
> Often, our military members do not know how to deal with civilian people, whether they are Department of Defense civilians, or their own service branch civilians—like Army—or people who are in commercial companies.

Sometimes we need to adjust the style of our interpersonal skills to the population we are working with. For example, we cannot order civilians around like we would our soldiers.

When working with young soldiers, you learn to be more directive in nature. They have to learn to respond immediately to your request as it will often save their life.

With civilians, and in an office environment, you need to spend more time explaining what needs to be done and why.

We need to adjust the style of our interpersonal skills to the population we are working with.

Another thing that people do not realize is that when you are building those relationships, it cannot just be on the surface. You must assess what it is within your own organization that could perhaps help that other organization in terms of dealing with a problem.

Or, you might need to develop an understanding of what each organization can do to help each other. Again, that is building relationships. You may say, "Here's an opportunity we have to work together. Here's where I think our organization could help yours."

Or, you may say, "You've got this capability. I think we could use your expertise to help us."

I asked, "How do you know ahead of time, *I need to develop a relationship with these types of companies or organizations?*"

As I would go back to the Pentagon, I would think about, *Who am I working with and who else might I need to work with?*

Some of it is nurturing relationships you just established with somebody within another service, or with an organization like the Defense Logistics Agency, or with an organization that you might have come from previously. Sometimes my boss would suggest that I should meet people within a specific organization.

Maybe there's a rift between your two organizations. If you have worked in that organization before and you already have a linkage there, maybe you can keep massaging that relationship to help the teams blend a little bit better. You start by figuring out the sticking points and then you lift those roadblocks.

After nurturing some of those relationships, we would come back and say, "Hey, we need to break down more barriers."

At USTRANSCOM we started a personnel exchange program for six months, where we would give some of our up-and-coming civilians growth opportunities. We would say, "For six months, you're going to swap with another person in a totally different organization."

Those folks would then go work in not only a totally different organization, but in a different service, with a totally different lingo and culture. Again, we were trying to build trust and leverage different ways to come up with solutions.

These other organizations were not the enemy. But there is always a fear in military organizations that someone is going to try to take your money, or your authority, or your people. So you put up walls. You don't share. That leads to a lack of trust because you haven't shared.

Another thing I think happens is that people do not afford themselves the opportunity to establish relationships before they need to leverage them. They wait until it is late in the game and then they will say, "Well, they are just going to have to come to me."

> **People do not afford themselves the opportunity to establish relationships before they need to leverage them. They wait until it is late in the game.**

When you are developing relationships, if you are walking around and talking to people and you are pleasant to be around, you can easily walk into social groups, see what's going on, and hear what's going on.

Then, when something important comes up that you may not have been aware of, you can say, "Oh? That meeting's at 4:00 and they're going to be talking about that? Would you mind if I come? I think our organization might be able to help yours."

You can easily get yourself into the meeting.

What you do not want to do is do it in the manner of, "What do you mean, you didn't have my section involved? I need to be there to ensure our organization is represented."

It's much more effective to instead say, "Our organization might be of value here. I think if we could talk about it, we could find a joint solution here."

There may be times when the boss will say, "The decision is already made."

You do not then want to say, "Well, we weren't consulted."

If you have not nurtured these relationships in advance, they are not even going to think to call you in.

You need to realize that everybody is always rushing to make things happen. If you have not nurtured these relationships in advance, they are not even going to think to call you in. Worse yet, they do not want to call you in because you are antagonistic.

Leading through influence is about technique.

REFLECTIONS:

Leadership through influence is all about establishing, maintaining, and nurturing positive, trusting, and caring relationships with people, regardless of whether they are within your span of control. The sooner you master this art, the more effective you will be as a leader. Most executive-level leaders have mastered the ability to positively influence the actions and decisions of others, both within and well beyond their span of control.

Much of leading through influence is about how you make others feel. When people know you care about them—

When people know you care about them—when they like, trust, and respect you—you will be far more able to have a positive influence on their actions and decisions.

when they like, trust, and respect you—you will be far more able to have a positive influence on their actions and decisions. If you treat others poorly, it will eventually come back to bite you.

The higher up the ladder one wishes to go, the more important it is to be proactive in terms of establishing and nurturing trusting, collaborative relationships with people at all levels, both internally and externally.

INTROSPECTIONS:

1   Think of someone you know who is especially effective at leading through influence. What behaviors do they exhibit that make them so effective at leading through influence? How do they treat others? How do they make others feel?

2   Think of a time when a successful outcome resulted from your own ability to lead through influence. What interpersonal skills did you leverage?

3   What is one thing you could modify about your own behavior toward others that might improve your ability to lead through influence?

TEN

Overcoming Gender Bias

There is still a challenge for women to be taken seriously. It is ongoing. We as women still must work a little harder, a little smarter, a bit more intentional than men to be treated equally, fairly, and with respect. There is still that challenge.

-MELISSA REIFF
Former Chairwoman and CEO, The Container Store

With the obvious exception of the event you read about in Chapter Two, for most of my nearly three-decade career in global technology enterprises, I honestly experienced very little gender bias. I do not mean to imply that there was no workplace gender bias, but for the most part, if it did exist where I was, I somehow managed to finesse around it.

In the early 1980s, the University of Rhode Island accepted me with open arms as one of a small minority of women into their MBA program. Most of my classmates with whom I carpooled were young, married men. I enjoyed being accepted as one of their valued friends and collaborators.

After graduation from MBA school, I was lucky that the Fortune 100s, in those days, had quota-based programs to hire and develop women for leadership. I was blessed to be selected, both at AT&T and at IBM, to participate in their truly outstanding management and leadership development programs. Timing was everything.

Along the way, I did have a few close encounters of the infuriating kind with certain macho men who seemed to take pleasure in making inappropriate remarks when women were around. I quickly learned to make sure my presence was known when I entered a room full of guys telling off-color jokes. I would usually say something like, "Okay, guys, recess is over now." Then I would smile sweetly, wink at them, take my seat, and change the subject. It did not take very long before their inappropriate remarks ceased to occur when they knew I was around.

I found things worked best for me when I was straightforward and acted as though I belonged in the room, because I *did* belong in the room. Likewise, I made it known to my manager when and why I believed I deserved a promotion or when I had a bright idea that could benefit the business. By doing so, I was treated as an equal by virtually all the men I worked with.

> **I found things worked best for me when I was straightforward and acted as though I belonged in the room, because I *did* belong in the room.**

Of course, there can always be an exception to keep us on our toes, like in my early days at IBM. I will never forget one particularly rude salesman who seemed to take great pleasure in looking down his nose at me as he towered above my petite frame. He made a habit of calling me "Honey," and more than once said to me, "Now don't you worry your pretty little head about this. I'll handle it."

Yes, I may have wanted to deck him, but it was clear to me that he acted like a jerk to everyone, not just toward me. Yet, it took me a while to figure that out. While I initially took it personally, I finally realized he was just a flat-out narcissist. As my dear friend, the renowned psychiatrist and author Mark Goulston, MD, once said, "You aren't going to change a narcissist. When he cannot create a win-lose situation in which you lose and he wins, he'll need to come up with something more workable."

I finally learned to just ignore him. When I saw him enter the office, I would engage myself with someone else, or I might leave the room, or make a phone call. I let the other guys in the office deal with him. He was simply not worth my time. How he succeeded as a salesman, I will never know.

That said, gender bias does exist. You have already read my story in Chapter Two about the gender bias that ultimately dealt the fatal blow to my corporate career. I should have known better at that point than to get caught up in such a situation, and I will now tell you why.

The Far End of the Table

Thanks to my experience leading a professional services organization at IBM, I occasionally received phone calls from headhunters, asking me to consider promotional opportunities in other global technology companies looking to establish their own professional services organizations. One recruiter called me several times about a chance to help establish a North American-based professional services organization for a global technology conglomerate headquartered in a different part of the world.

Having previously managed similar engagements, I was familiar with the kind of gender bias some international firms were known for at the time within their U.S. operations. So, I politely declined these invitations to interview with such firms. (I suspect much has changed for the better since then!) It was obvious to me that working for this particular conglomerate would not likely benefit my career.

Eventually, this headhunter came up with a different spin on his sales pitch. He made it clear that this U.S. division was run and managed by executives who were every bit as committed to the advancement of women in leadership as AT&T and IBM were. Skeptical, I finally agreed to at least meet with the U.S. division president and his direct reports for an initial conversation.

To make a long story short, I was delightfully surprised. Although, as with most technology companies at the time, there were few women in leadership there aside from the typical VP of HR, these executives were emphatic that they wanted to be more inclusive. In the end, I liked what I heard and believed what they said. They gave me an offer I could not refuse to establish and lead a new North American consulting practice. For the next three years, life was great.

During that time, I took on additional responsibilities. I took over a second professional services organization and served as the president's special projects chief. I sat at the right hand of the president at his

Although, as with most technology companies at the time, there were few women in leadership there aside from the typical VP of HR, these executives were emphatic that they wanted to be more inclusive.

weekly executive team meetings, and he usually asked me to weigh in on major decisions. I loved every minute of this job, until one day, the president announced his retirement.

Not surprisingly, the president named the sales VP as his replacement. I knew I would miss the president, but I got along great with the sales VP, as well as everyone else on the executive team. Once the new president was in place, things continued along just as before.

Then suddenly, out of the blue one Monday morning, a cadre of gray-suited executives descended from our global headquarters. For a solid week, these executives took over the boardroom. Our U.S.-based leaders were individually called into one meeting after another throughout that week. No one seemed to be smiling when they exited these meetings. I was not asked to participate in any of these meetings until that Friday when I was invited to attend the usual weekly executive team meeting.

As I walked into the meeting, the female VP of HR whispered to me to sit at the far end of the table, rather than sit in my usual seat, to the right of the president's chair. The meeting was brief. The most senior executive from global headquarters announced that our new division president, the former VP of sales, was no longer with the firm. An executive from headquarters was named as acting president, effective immediately. A team of executives from the global headquarters would be staying on to oversee operations for the foreseeable future until a new president could be named. I knew immediately that this would be the beginning of the end for me.

For the next few months, I continued to run my professional services organizations while the consultants from headquarters carried out an evaluation of our U.S.-based manufacturing operations. I continued to attend the weekly executive team meetings, but my seat remained at far end of the table. Input from me was clearly not welcome and never requested.

Hello, gender bias.

> **The only viable approach for me was to accept the situation for what it was and prepare to move on to bigger and better things where women had the opportunity to be all they could be.**

I quickly realized this would be the new norm and I would never overcome it. The only viable approach for me to accept the situation for what it was and prepare to move on to bigger and better things where women had theopportunity to be all they could be. I made my exit from the company as soon as I found a suitable position elsewhere, and never looked back.

When I interviewed our women on top in preparation for writing this book, I wanted to know if any of them had ever had to deal with gender bias. Their answers were not surprising.

Melissa Reiff
Former Chairwoman and CEO
The Container Store

Melissa Reiff had this to say when I asked her, "Did you ever encounter any gender bias, either in school or as you rose through the ranks?"

I never felt any discrimination, or any gender bias, or anything like that while I was growing up. I just did not—at all—until I was older.

I did start to feel some gender bias as a young adult, getting out into the workplace. It was not easy, but I was determined and just kind of ignored it, I think. I just did what I was going to do and plowed on through.

I was a little like Sheryl Sandberg with her *lean in* philosophy, but I had more of a "surround yourself with great people," "be open for opportunity," "be creative," "take initiative," "the cream rises," "your contributions will be recognized" mindset.

However, I do think that we, as women, still have a long way to go. Every year I learn more, whether it is in the boardroom or during other opportunities for engagement with other

We all face challenges in our interactions with peers, vendors, partners, and colleagues. The key is how we respond to these challenges and overcome them. That we can control.

industry leaders. We all face challenges in our interactions with peers, vendors, partners, and colleagues. The key is how we respond to these challenges and overcome them. That we can control.

I am proud of the way our company works with and interacts with our many vendors and other retail partners in whatever capacity. The important point is to treat our interactions— whatever they are—with respect and fairness.

But there is still a challenge for women to be taken seriously. It is ongoing. We as women *still* must work a little harder, a little smarter, a bit more intentional than men to be treated equally, fairly, and with respect. There is still that challenge.

If I am in a meeting and getting up to pour myself a cup of coffee, I am one of those who will say, "Who would like a cup of coffee? I'm happy to get you one!" And I am hopeful that anyone else would do the same, too, regardless of gender. If it doesn't occur, I might be prone to say to the next person, "Hey, would you mind grabbing me a cup, too?"

Some people just don't think about it. I do not think it is always intentional, but they just assume that *we* are supposed to get the coffee, or *we* are supposed to clean up the dishes, or things like that. I mean, it doesn't keep me up at night, but I'm very much aware of it. I try to make sure that I always respond in the appropriate way.

Being bullheaded or obnoxious does not pay civic ends. It just does not. We are not going to get what we deserve—and what we should have—by doing

Being bullheaded or obnoxious does not pay dividends. It just does not. We are not going to get what we deserve—and what we should have—by doing that.

that. That is when I believe, as women, we get a bad rap for being that way: "She's just being a bull," or, "She's obnoxious," or, "She's so strong-willed and strong-headed."

We have got to have finesse and be smarter. It should not have to be that way, but it is what it is. So, we must continue to be wise and *lean in,* as Sheryl Sandberg says, so we can get it done for us now, and for the generations ahead.

Nancy Howell Agee
President and CEO
Carilion Clinic

During my conversation with Nancy Agee, president and CEO of Carilion Clinic, I asked her if she ever fell victim to gender bias, or if she went through a metamorphosis when the word *chief* was added to her title.

I am not sure I went through a metamorphosis, but in some ways, I became aware that others now thought of me differently. That was a little surprising, especially becoming the CEO.

I heard it more in reference. First, I am a woman. It is not so much now, but at the time, it was unusual—and it's still sort of unusual. A colleague of mine said that a colleague of hers—somebody I knew—said, "Oh, they've just asked her to babysit. She'll be out of there in a year."

> **A colleague of mine said that a colleague of hers—somebody I knew—said, "Oh, they've just asked her to babysit. She'll be out of there in a year."**

It was a dismissive sort of thing, really referencing, "What is a woman doing in that job?"

I heard several people say, "You're the CEO? Well, you're a woman!"

I mean, even a very nice man said, "You have what job?"

He kept trying to diminish it, saying something like, "Oh, you mean you are over a department."

I did not introduce myself as the CEO, but somebody else had. This other person, a man, said, "She's the CEO of the whole organization."

Then he went, "But you're a woman!"

Incredulous, I commented, "He honestly said that?"

He did! I will never forget it. I was standing there, and I said, "Yeah, you're right," and then I said, "Gosh, I didn't realize that."

Then he laughed and I did, too, but it was unexpected.

I mentioned to Nancy a story told to me by a female division president of a major corporation. She had just taken over as head of the organization and was attending a company event where she was to address an audience of important clients. The attendees had come from all over the world, and they expected to meet the new president.

Before the formal meeting began, she entered the ballroom and casually walked about the room, greeting people. No one asked her who she was or what she did for a living. She was just chatting with them, saying things like, "How nice that you're here. Where are you from?"

When she went up on stage to be introduced as the new president, the men in the room, whom she had just talked to minutes before, almost fell over. They could not believe *she* was the president.

To that, Nancy remarked:

> Well, that has not been an uncommon experience for me, either.

I asked her, "Do you still continue to see that happen from time to time?"

> Much less so now, but it certainly does continue.

"That's interesting. How long have you been in the CEO role now?"

Almost ten years.

My husband is a judge. Not infrequently, when we attend events together, I will get questions like, "Oh, and what do you do?" or, "Oh, it must be nice to have some time with him when he's home"—his court is on a circuit—or, "Do you get to have a long vacation this summer?"

It is somewhat patronizing. I don't really know how to respond. I have to admit, sometimes I respond like, "Well, no. I am sort of busy. What do you do?" There is just a disconnect—which is unfortunate. It is less than it used to be, but it is still there.

> **There is just a disconnect—which is unfortunate. It is less than it used to be, but it is still there.**

I commented, "I suppose it may be a cultural thing. For so many years, organizations were run by men, particularly in healthcare. We women were brought up as little children hearing, "Girls are the nurses. Boys are the doctors."

Yes, I think that is true and I think we still are raised that way. In fact, I have a little grandson. He is almost two now, but I'm starting to read books to him. There is an effort to make books not biased, but they are, still.

Wendy Johnson
Former President and CEO
Dale Carnegie franchise, Atlanta, GA

Before she became the president and CEO of Dale Carnegie of
Georgia, Wendy Johnson worked in male-dominated
environments during her career in sales. Wendy highlighted a few
of her early experiences dealing with gender bias while she worked
for Martin Marietta, selling metals to manufacturing companies
like Boeing, Kenworth Trucks, Peterbilt Motors Company, and big
irrigation companies.

> It took me three months to get my first sales order. These
> companies would just literally slam the door when I called on
> them. They would not see me because I was a woman.
>
> When I first came into the job, the men I sold to—my clients—
> apparently felt like their life had been ruined now that their
> vendor was a woman. They figured they were going to miss
> out on all their two-martini lunches because they did not want
> to get into trouble. After all, part of their relationship with
> their vendors was the social part—drinking lunches, golf, and
> fishing trips.
>
> I finally realized that the only way to successfully break in and
> win their business was to take these guys out for a drinking
> lunch. I had to show them that I was fun. So, I would take them
> out to lunch to those sleazebag bars with the double martinis.
> They would get a double martini.
>
> What they did not know was that I would go into the
> restaurant prior to the time of our reservation. I would tell the

waitstaff to only serve me drinks without any alcohol, because I just could not have the alcohol. But the customers never knew that.

So, I started being fun. I decided to do what the salesmen would do. I would take these clients out on fishing trips. My company helped me arrange salmon fishing trips off the coast of Oregon or Washington. I must admit, it was hard.

I decided to do what the salesmen would do...I must admit, it was hard.

I remember my experience selling to Kenworth Trucks and Peterbilt Motors Company. At least they had a woman purchasing agent. At one point, both of our companies wanted us to go down to Dallas together to the big truck show. So, she and I went to this convention together. We went into the big hall where these huge trucks were on display, you know, like a car show or a boat show.

She and I walked the floor together. Of course, in front of every truck was a woman in a swimsuit. As we walked by these swimsuit-clad women—and we were in our business suits and carrying our briefcases—these women were clearly embarrassed. Boy, was that a male-dominated industry.

I must say, Wendy's story brought back vivid memories to me, memories I had almost forgotten about. Back when I first began my career in technology sales—forty years ago—I remember attending dozens of the world's largest technology industry tradeshows. It was very typical back then, for the smaller vendors especially, to employ scantily clad models to stand in front of their booths, handing out candy or cookies or drink tickets to an after-show get-together, just to lure in hordes of businessmen to visit the booth. I would think to myself, *That's pretty low class*, but it was so common, and it worked like magic. These little companies successfully reeled in lots of male buyers to listen to their sales pitch.

Of course, Fortune 100 companies, at least the ones I worked for like AT&T and IBM, had huge, opulent vendor displays smack in the center of the convention showcase area. Our booths were so enormous, we naturally drew the attention of most everyone without ever resorting to such questionable attention-getting tactics.

These kinds of tactics can still be found in a few industries. While trade shows in such industries may not feature swimsuit-clad women these days, some companies still feature exquisitely beautiful female actresses or models, clad in skintight attire or very short skirts, to point out the features of the company's newest products. It is all about getting the buyer's attention—and it works.

This is not so different from Hollywood. Consider how some actresses are dressed as they strut their stuff down the red carpet at the Academy Awards or other awards ceremonies these days. They do get attention, don't they?

Then, Wendy continued:

I do not want to leave you with the impression that the only way I could ever get accepted into this male-dominated business environment was to drink and go on fishing trips with my customers. They did eventually begin to appreciate me for what I had to offer—what differentiated me from my male counterparts. I provided service, every bit as good, if not even better, than my male counterparts did. I cared about, understood, and anticipated the details, every bit as well, if not even better, than my male counterparts did. When something went wrong, I was all over it, every bit as quickly, if not even faster, than my male counterparts. I went out of my way to be even more attentive than my male counterparts. Women have a very special value-add to business transactions. The customers recognized this over time.

Women have a very special value-add to business transactions. The customers recognized this over time.

It is said that the true value of a client-vendor relationship only becomes apparent when there are issues to be resolved. How a vendor recovers from problems is what builds client-vendor trust and solidifies the relationship.

Later in my career, I was excited about owning a Dale Carnegie franchise because I had the freedom to create what I wanted, in a market that I wanted to be a part of. I eventually chose to make women one of my main areas of focus.

The reason I began to focus on women was because whenever I would walk into our classroom, I usually found two-thirds to three-quarters of the students in the class were men. I always wondered, *Why is this?*

This went on for eighteen years. And now that I'm gone, I hear it's still that way.

Once I finally got my feet on the ground as a franchise owner and I was feeling perky running the show, I felt more confident that I could take the risk of putting together a women's program. This was only a risk because I knew there would be a smaller prospect base. I knew I would have to focus on selling to women's leadership groups and the few human resources professionals who oversaw diversity programs within the organization.

Once they found out how expensive the Dale Carnegie training was, their interest would disappear because executive-level leadership within these organizations simply would not fund the program for their women. They would talk the talk about developing a leadership path for women, but they would not walk the walk. It was very interesting.

They would talk the talk about developing a leadership path for women, but they would not walk the walk.

The more we studied it, we determined the reason women were not getting selected to participate in the class was multifactorial. One reason was that women did not ask for development training. Instead, they were biding their time, waiting to be tapped.

It became evident that companies were simply not developing their women or putting them in development programs to get them ready for leadership roles. It was only when, at some point, someone inside or outside the company might start looking at their diversity statistics and would then say, "Oh, we've got to promote some more women."

Only then would they select some woman who was consistent, who really worked hard, and who knew their products. They'd say, "Hey, this person might really be good. They are very reliable. We can put them in a new role," but they still would not give them any leadership development training, so they had a high potential to fail. This was so typical.

Bottom line, it came down to three issues: One, there was an unconscious bias by the male executives. Two, there were women who had no vision for themselves. Three, we determined that some women were not advancing within their organizations because they did not behave like they were worthy of development—they did not display an executive presence and they didn't have a voice that got the attention of their coworkers or executive leadership.

So, we felt we needed to create a program that could help women establish their own personal leadership style or brand. We wanted to give them a voice. We wanted to help these women learn problem-solving and innovation, and all the other attributes

We felt we needed to create a program that could help women establish their own personal leadership style or brand. We wanted to give them a voice.

that companies look for when promoting from within.

I asked Wendy, "When you said *they didn't have a voice,* was it because they were afraid to say anything, or did they believe they weren't in a position that was worthy of being listened to?"

Well, it was a little bit of all of that. One thing we found was that some women are not confident enough to speak up. We also discovered that some women's voices are not strong enough, or well developed enough, to get the attention they deserve.

Of course, there is this unconscious bias that men have. Men tend to think of other men first before they consider putting a woman up for promotion, unless they are told that they must recommend a woman.

"Did you find that most of the men who went through the Dale Carnegie program proactively asked to attend, or did they somehow get the attention of a senior leader who said, 'This guy has got potential, but he is a little rough. We need to send him to that program to develop him'?"

I think it's a little of both. We found that men were more likely to ask. But I also think, most of the time, men are put on a track.

We are at a point, now, where women are finally being more readily identified for promotion. Yet, I know there is still a deficit of women in the C-suite.

Even now, when people get on an airplane, if the captain standing there to greet them is a woman, some passengers comment, "Hmmm. It's a woman captain on this plane."

Some people are still worried about that.

I commented, "Yes. I have a lovely female friend who has been a pilot for American Airlines for almost thirty years. She told me, 'To this day, when people see me in an airport, they assume I'm a flight attendant, even though I'm dressed in a pilot's uniform.'"

When I told people I sold aluminum, they immediately thought I was simply selling siding to construction sites, but instead I was selling to Boeing! I was selling to Kenworth Trucks and Peterbilt Motors Company. They assumed that I could not possibly have a big industrial position. They figured I just had some little, low-level, decorative sort of position. There were always these assumptions.

When I first started my sales management career, I do not know how many times I would travel with my salesmen to customer calls. The customer would only look at my sales guy and talk to him. They would not even look at me. They got it completely reversed.

The realization would only come when we would begin to have a price controversy or a discussion that required my input or my approval, as the sales manager. Then my salesman would say, "Well, we will have to talk to Wendy, my boss. She's the one who has the last word on pricing."

At that point, I would look at the customer and smile. I could tell they were thinking, *Oh, my God. I've got this reversed*. It was just their assumption. It was subliminal. I am not sure people were intentionally discriminatory. It was just not what they were accustomed to.

Lieutenant General Kathleen M. Gainey
U.S. Army, Retired

I asked Lt. Gen. Kathy Gainey, "Was it difficult for you, as a junior officer, to go into an environment where, not only were you junior to most everybody, but you were also a woman? Did you struggle with that to an extent that might have been different from how a man would deal with being junior?"

I am sure being junior was an issue—you do not know what you do not know. Of course, I was unsure of myself, but I think male platoon leaders had the same challenges. Women were new to these units so that did bring additional challenges.

Now, being some of the first women, you had the issues with guys making catcalls. You had the issues of men making inappropriate comments. Because women were just starting to come into these units, we gals would ask our fellow female platoon leaders, "How are you dealing with all this?"

> **What I learned to do was based on advice given to me by a fellow female officer who said, "If you see it and you can stop it, then confront it. If you *hear* it, but you cannot see who is doing it, then ignore it."**

What I learned to do was based on advice given to me by a fellow female officer who said, "If you see it and you can stop it, then confront it. If you *hear* it, but you cannot see who is doing it, then ignore it. Just make them yell louder, as though you do not even hear it at all—as though you are deeply focused on a conversation, or you are taking notes or whatever. Act as though you never even heard it. You do not want them to think you are just walking by, doing nothing about it. But if you cannot pinpoint who it is, you would just be chasing a phantom."

I asked, "Were there other things working against you, as a woman, that men didn't have to struggle with?"

Yes. I came into the Army in 1978. You may remember, it used to be that when you got pregnant, you had to get out of the military. That rule had only just changed in 1975. So, all the women who came before us, if they got pregnant, they had to get out.

It also used to be that when you got married, you had to get out. Then they relaxed that rule to just, if you had a child you had to get out. So my fellow female officers didn't have the luxury of having many female role models who were married women with kids.

When I got to the battalion, we only had four women platoon leaders. When I left, we had fifteen. Suddenly, our platoon leaders were predominately women, not men. This was because women could only go to organizations that were not scheduled to be in combat—on the front line.

When I came in, I could not even go to the platoon they had assigned me to because they could not accept women. It was not that the unit would refuse women. They could not accommodate women because it was a heavy equipment transport company and there were no temporary billets (lodging quarters) for women when they would arrive at tactical units.

Just to clarify, these units moved large pieces of equipment that belonged to the infantry, armor, and engineer units. The unit I was assigned to would bring in our trucks the day before, and then they would load up the equipment the next morning and depart. The male soldiers would sleep in the transient barracks.

So, the infantry and armor officers said, "We can't have any women in these transportation units because we don't have any barracks for women." Of course, there was no bathroom or shower for women, either.

Since the women could not be assigned to their divisional units, the Army then placed them in what was called theater-level units, which was the 37th Transportation Group.

Finally, Colonel Brown, the 37th Transportation Group commander, told the combat arms commanders, "We are going to have to change things, guys. You have got to create some barracks space for women because I do not have a choice anymore. I am being assigned more female soldiers and platoon leaders in all my units.

"You are simply not going to get any more trucks until you find some barracks space for the women. I have to have proper billeting for all my platoon leaders and truck drivers."

Now, when you tell people that today, they do not believe it. They go, "That didn't happen."

Well, yes, it did!

I asked, "Is it a different military today?"

It is totally different. Now there is no field of expertise that women cannot be in.

Back then, they had just started breaking the mold by putting women in as engineers and in air defense artillery. And that was just, "Oh, my gosh!"

But then, women could only advance so far in those fields because they could not be assigned to units that were in direct support of the combat arms units.

Take Deb Lewis, for example, the retired colonel you interviewed in your first two books. Deb could not be in the combat engineers. Retired Lt. Col. Carol Barkalow could only be in a certain type of air defense artillery unit. She could not even *aspire* to be a battalion commander because she could not have had all the jobs required to develop her as a leader. That is why she switched and became a transportation officer. Now, there's nothing women can't do.

Now, there's nothing women can't do.

I then asked General Gainey, "When you came into the Army and went the route you did, were you put on a path that enabled you to make senior officer versus if you had been an engineer?"

Absolutely, because as female transportation officers, there were only a few jobs that were closed to us. Frankly, I did not even realize this back then. I was very lucky in that the transportation branch, overall, was very welcoming to women.

Some branches, such as ordnance and signal, were not very supportive of women. My female peers there related that

these branches were not very nurturing or encouraging.
I had nearly all male mentors. We did not have *any* women to
mentor us at all until much later. For most of my career, I had
all male mentors. Fortunately, these men would encourage
me. They gave me confidence, and they helped get me into
the good jobs.

"So today, women aren't restricted from anything?"

Nothing is restricted in the Army anymore. Today, the sky is
the limit.

"No reason you can't be a five-star?"

Well, we do not have any five-star generals anymore. Four-star
is as high as we go now. But there is no reason why a woman
cannot be a four-star and the chief-of-staff of the Army.

REFLECTIONS:

Despite all the diversity, inclusion, and equity programs in the
workplace today, gender bias continues to exist, and it likely always
will. Biases are a fact of life because we all come from different
perspectives and paradigms. Virtually everyone has biases, even
you and me.

We must face the fact that the only behaviors, beliefs, and biases
we can control are our own. While it is possible to influence
others, each of us must be allowed to come to our own conclusions
in our own time. None of us, individually or as a collective, can

force others to change their beliefs or values and expect to have a positive outcome. Human nature simply does not work that way.

Forcing another to adapt their beliefs to accommodate us, in my humble opinion, only serves to foster resentment and build walls. The current focus on mandated equity and inclusion, along with the downsides evident of the seemingly justified Me Too

> **None of us, individually or as a collective, can force others to change their beliefs or values and expect to have a positive outcome. Human nature simply does not work that way.**

movement, have unfortunately driven people away from willingly serving as mentors to those who most desperately need the mentoring. It has caused people to walk on eggshells. It prevents us from discussing what should be discussed, lest someone be offended. This is not in anyone's best interest, and it surely doesn't help women.

I am not saying we must do like Wendy Johnson did and take men on fishing trips or expect men to pursue our favorite pastimes with us. Rather, we should flex our communications styles to whatever it is that will be received well by the other person. Learn to ask meaningful questions and listen with the intent to understand the needs

> **Learn to ask meaningful questions and listen with the intent to understand the needs and objectives of others, regardless of gender. Serve as a role model.**

and objectives of others, regardless of gender. Serve as a role model.

Endeavor to conduct open, honest, and professional dialogs that will help others become the best version of themselves. Be willing to share your ideas. Become an indispensable ally—and maintain your sense of humor in the process.

Above all, recognize and accept those situations when no matter what you do, it may simply not be possible to overcome someone's gender bias. Simply do your best to be a value-added contributor, but when your ideas and input are not appreciated, then pick up your toys and find another playground where you can be more effective.

I love the quote by the late Jack Welch, former CEO and chairman of General Electric, "Face reality as it is, not how you wish it to be."

Life is too short to spin your wheels trying to force fit yourself into a place where you will never be welcome. Instead, be discerning enough to know when you can have a positive impact versus when you cannot. When you cannot, then simply move on to wherever you can be at your best. Hopefully, based on what you now know, you will be able to be that bright, shining superstar right where you are right now.

In the meantime, never assume anyone is biased against you. Instead, assume you are a highly valued member of the team, and you more than likely will be.

INTROSPECTIONS:

1. Have you ever experienced gender bias? If so:
    a. What happened and how did you handle it?
    b. Were you happy with the outcome?
    c. Based on what you know now, if you could have a do-over with that experience, what would you do differently?

2. Do you have a female role model who seems at ease and adept in terms of working collaboratively with men? If so, have you asked her to mentor you?

3. Have you ever had a male mentor? If so:
    a. Did you listen to them and consider their advice?
    b. What was it that made that mentoring relationship work or not work for you?
    c. What did you learn from the experience?

ELEVEN

Self-Development

I have always tried to frighten myself a little bit every day. I push myself a little bit harder to do things at which I expect to fail, but which are not existential threats. I try to de-risk life by taking small, calculated risks that demystify failure. In that way, I am able to enjoy life, even during periods of uncertainty.

-KERRY HEALEY, PHD

Inaugural President, Milken Center for Advancing the American Dream

Back when I first took what was then called Gallup's StrengthsFinder 2.0 assessment, I was not surprised to discover that "Learner" was one of my top-three strengths. The assessment results read:

> You love to learn. The process, more than the content or the result, is especially exciting for you. You are energized by the steady and deliberate journey from ignorance to competence. Your excitement leads you to engage in adult learning experiences. It enables you to thrive in dynamic work environments where you are asked to take on short project assignments and are expected to learn a lot about the new subject matter in a short period of time and then move on to the next one.

Yep, that describes me perfectly. Self-development and continuous learning are ways of life for me.

Regardless of whether "Learner" is one of your top strengths, having a proclivity for lifelong learning and self-development is vital for anyone who desires to rise to the C-suite.

No one enters any new role, in the C-suite or elsewhere, knowing everything they will need to know for the job. Even CEOs and board chairs have knowledge and skill gaps, even after years in the role. People, places, things, technologies, and situations change constantly. What you knew yesterday will be outdated by tomorrow. Successful leaders forever strive to keep learning and growing.

What you knew yesterday will be outdated by tomorrow. Successful leaders forever strive to keep learning and growing.

As mentioned in previous chapters, I had the privilege of participating in formal in-house sales training and leadership development programs provided by the Fortune 100 companies I worked for early in my career. I was also fortunate to have had the budget to attend external training put on by a host of third-party training companies, business partners, vendors, governmental organizations, and industry associations.

I have also been blessed to have had a couple of wonderful mentors over the years, my husband being one. Another came very early in my career, an older gentleman who had been a highly respected engineer with the Bell System seemingly forever. In my eyes, he knew everything. If, after doing all the research I could do on some technical challenge, I was still stymied, I never hesitated to schedule time with him, to help me understand. I have no doubt that my first promotion to the area technical support staff was thanks to his recommending me for that promotion, due to my tenacity and desire to learn.

Later in my career, I never passed up an opportunity to speak at conferences and industry association events. One reason for this was that, in return for speaking, I had the chance to attend all the other speakers' sessions, on a wide variety of topics. Thanks to that, I got to learn a great deal about all kinds of subjects on which I otherwise would likely have never taken the time to educate myself.

Just as I have done to write *Women on Top* and my previous two leadership books, I routinely go out of my way to seek the perspectives and insights of leaders and experts from various industries and disparate walks of life, the world over. Doing so has always paid dividends. I find virtually everyone I meet to be amazing. It is incredible what I can learn from just about anyone.

Sometimes I simply come away thinking, *Yeah, I thought I knew that.* Occasionally I am dumbfounded, especially when I have a preconceived but misinformed notion about some issue. You stand to learn a great deal by simply keeping an open mind.

Venturing Outside Your Circle Pays Off

In addition to attending cooking classes and performing arts programs together, some years ago my husband and I attended the Citizen's Police Academy put on by our local police department. Talk about seeing things from a whole new perspective! We found, just by walking a tiny portion of a mile in their shoes, we developed a completely new appreciation for what these highly trained professionals do. It was way more than we ever expected.

Moreover, we met an entirely new set of people who lived in our town. Everyone had an interesting career and intriguing outside interests. I have called on some of those individuals to pick their brains on a variety of topics in the years since.

Getting to know people outside your normal social and business circles can pay dividends, in ways you might never imagine.

Getting to know people outside your normal social and business circles can pay dividends, in ways you might never imagine.

I have always been a voracious reader. Throughout my career, I've had the opportunity to fly coast-to-coast on business trips more times than I could count. I always take a stack of trade magazines or leadership books to read on these flights. I still have bookshelves full of leadership books in my office, both new and old books with dog-eared pages marked with yellow highlighter, which I still refer to regularly, to this very day.

I especially love to read non-fiction. Ever since my childhood, and perhaps because of my British ancestry, I have always loved reading British history and historical novels. One of my all-time favorite reads was *The Diary of Samuel Pepys*. I found Pepys' diary—his own private daily journal—quite fascinating.

During the reign of England's Charles II and James II, Samuel Pepys was secretary to the British Admiralty, a leadership role somewhat like a Cabinet-level position today. Reading through his ten years of journal entries, from January 1, 1660, until May 31, 1669, I found Pepys to be a rather humble and pragmatic heartfelt leader.

Thanks to his sparkling wit and sense of humor, I came to realize that people are people. Always have been; always will be. Men and women were not that much different five hundred years ago than we are now. Our most basic wants, needs, concerns, and apprehensions have remained much the same for centuries. While customs, science, and technologies may have changed dramatically, that is about it. People, the world over, back then as well as now, have far more in common than not.

When you think about it, learning about and understanding the human psyche and motivations is key to being a great leader, in the C-suite and elsewhere. The most important thing to recognize, no matter how much you think you know, or how many degrees you may have, no one ever knows it all.

No matter how much you think you know, or how many degrees you may have, no one ever knows it all.

But that is what makes self-development such a fabulous journey. There is always more out there to learn and be amazed at, no matter where you look.

I was especially eager to discover what our seven amazing women on top have done and currently do in terms of self-development.

Jodi Berg
President and CEO
Vita-Mix Corporation

Knowing that Jodi Berg has a PhD as well as an MBA, I was intrigued to hear her perspectives on the value of learning.

I truly believe all of us are a melting pot of the things that we allow to be put into our pot. I am not 100 percent sure of where I started with this value, but I have been very, very selective during my lifetime about what I chose to put in my pot. When somebody would say something negative or discouraging, I would say, "Well, I'm not putting *that* in my pot."

I very selectively made sure that the things that I chose to live by were things that I loved in other people. If I would hear somebody speak and realize, *I love how they made me feel,* I would hear myself saying, "I want to make other people feel that way." That is how I became the melting pot of who I am today.

> **I very selectively made sure that the things that I chose to live by were things that I loved in other people.**

One of the things that was an incredibly important "Y" in the road for me was this: When I was growing up, I spent a lot of time looking for those people who were having a meaningful impact on other people. Understanding what that was, I was absorbing it and thinking, *I'm a sponge. I'm going to help myself grow and develop into the person I want to be, someone I'll feel really good about.*

Hopefully, other people will get the benefit that I have gotten from others.

Nancy Howell Agee
President and CEO
Carilion Clinic

While interviewing Nancy Agee, I asked her what it was that kick-started her leadership career and how she made the transition from nursing.

I met a physician who became a mentor of mine, right here in Roanoke, years ago. I came to know him while attending medical grand rounds.

For those who do not know what *medical grand rounds* are, let me explain. Medical grand rounds are kind of a highest-level educational activity for residents, fellows, practicing physicians, and faculty. There are grand rounds in every specialty—pediatrics, obstetrics, and so on. Medical grand rounds are kind of the top dog.

So, there I was, a staff nurse. I typically would not have been invited to attend medical grand rounds, so I just started showing up there because I thought it was interesting.

He was responsible for medical grand rounds.

I asked Nancy to clarify, "Was this like a symposium?"

Yes, it was a weekly symposium. There were about 200 people, almost all physicians, and back in the day, almost all men.

Anyway, I just started going, and he noticed that I was there, like an ugly duckling—you know, in the wrong place. Then, occasionally, as the day's program was over, he would walk out with me.

We started chatting, and then I would ask him questions. At some point, one of the grand rounds was called the *Clinical Pathology Conference*. It was a conference where the facts of the case were presented "absent one"—one fact. Three residents would have to develop a differential diagnosis and explain what they thought the actual diagnosis would be.

I thought that was fascinating. It was like putting a puzzle together. He started asking me to present my thoughts on it, which was scary to me.

"That had to be a little intimidating since you were a nurse, there with all doctors."

It was completely intimidating.

But it was also an example of the fact that he was not trying to embarrass me. Instead, he wanted to stimulate my curiosity and give me the confidence that I knew something—that I could show others that we all had things to offer to healthcare.

> **He wanted to stimulate my curiosity and give me the confidence that I knew something—that I could show others that we all had things to offer.**

So, that is how we became friends. His background was in oncology. My interest was in oncology. So, we began to talk about it and the rest is history.

"Were you the only nurse at these events?"

Yes.

"You must have stood out there, being one of the few women, if not the *only* woman there."

Yes. People still remember it. They still make comments like, "I remember when you used to do that."

"Even just making the decision to *attend* one of those events might have been somewhat intimidating. Why did you step up to attend? Did you have a conversation with anyone and ask, 'Hey, would this be okay?' Or did you just go?"

I just went.

I then asked Nancy if there were other things that she did to develop her business acumen, beyond the typical healthcare system-related management issues.

I'll give you two different situations, two different scenarios.

Early on, when I was still young in my career, I got involved in the American Cancer Society. That was a natural interest. But that opened so many new doors for me, wherein I met business leaders from all over, as well as community leaders who were raising money, who were offering transportation, who were CEOs or business leaders from other companies.

After a couple of years of volunteering for the organization, I became a member of the board—at a very young age—and got to develop a network. That proved important over time.

> **I became a member of the board—at a very young age—and got to develop a network. That proved important over time.**

The other organization that I got involved in, kind of as a lark, was the local community theater. I am not an actor or a singer or a dancer. But I liked working in the back. I liked seeing what was going on. So I volunteered. I helped with makeup and helped with anything they needed, like building scenery.

Again, I became a member of that board. I created a different network with different people who were interested in the arts, and who were also philanthropic and business leaders.

These were great opportunities. They, then, proved to be instrumental in helping me, too. Those are just some practical things you can do that are also fun and can enable you to create different networks that can be supportive of you in your career.

I then asked Nancy if she learned about managing corporate finances after she entered the C-suite.

No, no, no. It was way sooner than that. Maybe it goes all the way back to the grant-writing, building on that. That was one of the things that I needed to learn back then.

"Of course, you've got to continue to evolve and keep learning."

Yeah, totally. I seek feedback. I still do. Every year I ask employees, "I'd love to have your feedback."

"Whom do you go to for feedback?"

My two go-tos are (1) my chief administrative officer, who is an amazing coach and a very thoughtful woman. She is just terrific at giving feedback and very genuine. And (2) my board chair, who is very supportive, very encouraging, completely understanding, and has very high expectations. When he doesn't like something, he's very clear about it.

Linda Rutherford
Senior Vice President, Chief Communications Officer
Southwest Airlines

When I asked Linda Rutherford, "What do you think was the key differentiator that set you apart on your way to reaching the top?" she said this:

> First of all, I don't like the whole "reaching the top" phrase. I don't feel like this is a destination. I feel like it's a journey. Maybe I will master something, or I will get good at something, but then there is always something else I want to know or do.
>
> I feel like it's this mountain you just keep climbing forever.

"Thank you for sharing that. What have been some of your more significant career development challenges?"

I feel like I got my MBA by just digging in and trying to learn the business as best I could.

The challenge driven by the COVID-19-related travel restrictions has just been awesome. I feel like I got my MBA by just digging in and trying to learn the business as best I could.

Of course, we've had great partners. I will ask our managing director of investor relations a thousand questions. He is very patient with me. Over the years, I have spent intentional time studying our balance sheets, our profit-and-loss statements, and our earnings reports to try and understand all of that.

In fact, I was talking to a professor at DePaul University. His name is Matt Ragas. He just wrote a book with a colleague called *Business Acumen for Strategic Communicators*. He was like, "You're my poster child! You're that person who was the communicator but had to learn the business. You could give advice to people who are up-and-coming in the communications profession."

It was kind of fun to think through what some of those challenges were. Again, you just don't stop learning. If I stopped learning the moment I left school, I'd still be on a typewriter and I'd still have a giant brick of a phone. You would worry about being irrelevant pretty quickly. You have to be a lifelong learner.

> **You just don't stop learning... You would worry about being irrelevant pretty quickly. You have to be a lifelong learner.**

I then asked, "Did you have any kind of leadership training through Southwest or outside the company? Or has it mostly been on-the-job training?"

It was a little bit of both. I was able to go to some outside learnings. I went to a short course at Harvard. We have what we call the Southwest Airlines University, so we have internal learning and development. They had several leadership classes, and they were terrific. They are really focused on how to unlock the potential of your team—what things you need to do to understand what each person brings to the table.

Today, that would be our version of Gallup's StrengthsFinders—that we support in our organization. Back then, I think it was called "Alligator Alley." The whole idea was to avoid the alligators in the swamp. You had to work together to figure out how to constantly cross the swamp—that was the analogy. It was really good.

So, yes, it was a combination of learning outside the organization and then learning through our internal courses at SWA University.

Kerry Healey
Inaugural President
Milken Center for Advancing the American Dream

I asked Kerry Healey, PhD, the former lieutenant governor of Massachusetts and now president of the Milken Center for Advancing the American Dream, about her decision to run for public office for the first time.

"When you made that decision to step out and run for office, it meant you were going to have to do fundraising and a bevy of things that a lot of people might never even consider. When you realized what all was involved, did you ever think to yourself, *Oh, my gosh! How am I going to do that?* Did you seek out people who had done those kinds of things before, for coaching and guidance?"

No! That is the one thing that I find quite interesting about all these discussions about leadership. I never had mentors. I never knew anyone who was on the path I wanted to travel. So, no.

There were a lot of really bad learning experiences. Early on, when I was starting my first campaign as state representative, I literally went to the secretary of state's office in the state house. I looked up where the state house was and went in there. They have a little bookshop, and they have a book that's called *How to Run for Office*.

I remember purchasing the pamphlet. It has a checklist in the back of it that says, "You have to open a bank account. You have to fill out these forms. You must do this and that, and the other thing. Then, to become a candidate, you have to collect this many signatures."

That's how I first ran for office! I did not live in Massachusetts until fairly recently before I ran for office. I was not involved with the party at all before that. I needed to go register with a party. I didn't really know that many people outside my local mothers' group. It was a huge leap.

I commented, "When most people run for office, they don't typically win the first time out."

Nor did I.

"New entrants in politics don't have brand recognition. Nobody knows who they are unless they've been on television, or in the news or whatever. Maybe then people recognize them. That is a challenge that a lot of women would be fearful of, taking that kind of a step. Many women would immediately think, *I can't succeed at this, so I won't even start.*"

Well, I knew I was going to lose. But I also knew that I would learn a lot by doing it.

It wasn't that I didn't run full force. I absolutely did. I was deeply, deeply disappointed that I didn't win. But I knew I wasn't going to win. I just knew it was absolutely impossible for me to win.

For one thing, there were only 13 percent registered Republicans in Massachusetts. There were a certain number of Independents, but the vast majority were Democrats. So, the probability of my winning was so small.

"But then you did it again."

I did, two years later. But, in the meantime, I got involved with the party. Then I eventually ran the party.

Once I chaired the party, I realized, *Okay. We're not going to win with the followers that we have. I need to build a new base. I need to rebuild the party, and I need to rebrand it to make it viable.*

I have always tried to frighten myself a little bit every day. I push myself a little bit harder to do things at which I expect to fail, but which are not existential threats. I try to de-risk life by taking small, calculated risks that demystify failure. In that way, I am able to enjoy life, even during periods of uncertainty.

You must be comfortable operating in environments where there are a lot of variables that you simply cannot control.

I think living amicably with ambiguity is one of the things that leaders must do. You must be comfortable operating in environments where there are a lot of variables that you simply cannot control. You must find a way to *not* worry about those things but still account for them. I do not ruminate.

I do not worry about what most people think. Instead, I surround myself with a group of people whose opinions I respect.

If those people, my inner circle of friends and family whom I deeply respect, were to come to me and say, "We're concerned about this or we don't like this thing that you're doing," I would take it very, very seriously and I would make changes.

Even after my experience running for governor, I felt like I still viewed the press and the whole process of media as being very alien and hostile. So, I founded a little television company and shot a TV series called *Shining City,* which was seen by almost no one. But it was good for me to have the opportunity to be on the other side of the interview, to be an interviewer as opposed to the person who was being peppered with questions. It allowed me to control all the aspects of the lighting, the sound, the set, the cutting, the editing. That made me feel much more comfortable.

It did not really matter to me that the show was not a huge success and did not go on to become a permanent series. What mattered to me was that I had learned how to control the medium. I taught myself not to be nervous on camera anymore.

I asked Kerry, "You didn't hire someone to coach you on what to do in front of a camera or what to do when you were being interviewed or asked questions?"

I started out as a policy writer, and that was hard from the standpoint that I had to develop ideas, but also relatively easy because I had a long time to perfect them and no one could see or hear me. When I was thrown into the world of television in politics, I really wasn't prepared for a three-dimensional type of communication—expressing ideas while being heard and seen. Even after I had overcome my fear of being seen on television, I still wanted to work on effectively communicating as a speaker.

I did hire a coach once. I hired a Shakespearean acting coach to help me with my voice—I had a job reading essays I had written on the radio. I didn't like the way my voice sounded. So the coach helped me figure to out how to modulate my voice.

"Do you have any little hints? What kinds of things did they tell you?"

It's all about breathing.

"It's like singing?"

Yes, it is a lot like singing.

Wendy Johnson
Former President and CEO
Dale Carnegie franchise, Atlanta, GA

I asked Wendy Johnson, "When you took over the company, how did you learn what you needed to know? Did you have a deer-in-headlights moment like, *Oh, my gosh. How am I going to run this thing myself?*"

Yes, I was a deer in headlights.

Fortunately, I had handpicked a controller whom   aligned with really well. She wasn't college educated, but she was a grassroots kind of person who had worked in tenuous situations before.

I was dealing with a serious lack of money. The inability to pay taxes and payroll can kind of scare most people off. When I hired her, I said, "Things are going to get ugly. I may be asking my partner to leave. You'll have to be tough, and we're going to have to be creative. If you think you will get scared by this, then you can't work here."

She said, "Oh, no. I've been through hell. I know what it's like."

"Well, have you ever had to put payroll on a credit card?"

"Oh, yes!"

"Okay then!"

So together, she and I figured it out. We learned QuickBooks and we dealt with all the tax, payroll, and financial juggling. We worked hand-in-hand.

I am going to be honest with you. If we did not know the answer, we Googled it. Each time I looked for help on the internet or called my CPA, I learned more about how to run a business.

If we did not know the answer, we Googled it.

We ran the business using the internet, Rocket Lawyer, and we found other Dale Carnegie franchisees who were willing to serve as mentors to us. Thank goodness people love to help!

I replied, "That's what a lot of entrepreneurial people do. Some of the biggest names in the business world got started doing just that. Look at Bill Gates's story, back in the early days of Microsoft. So much of that business, early on, was *seat of the pants* and *make it up as you go* management. As a business owner, you just have to fill in the gaps the best you can. As an entrepreneur, you have to be willing to take risks and do the best you can with what you have. When you don't have the things you need, you make it up and go from there."

Yeah. Yeah! I made a lot of mistakes because I did not get any training from any company I worked for, except Martin Marietta—and that was mainly product knowledge.

I didn't have a coach or a mentor. There were a couple of bosses who were awesome and were a good influence over my development. I have never forgotten them.

Over the years, I have had a few bad managers, but bad managers can be valuable, too. I would say to myself, *This is what it feels like being managed by somebody who's a bad manager. This doesn't feel good at all. I definitely won't repeat this when I have the opportunity to lead.*

Learning experiences can be good and bad. While experiencing a bad manager can be enlightening, it can also be at the root of a dysfunctional team. Studies show that the main reason people leave an organization is a lack of respect and the inability to work with their supervisor.

Studies show that the main reason people leave an organization is a lack of respect and the inability to work with their supervisor.

I replied, "Absolutely. I refined my own leadership skills and probably learned more from bad managers, because I never wanted to put other people in the position of feeling like I did because of how a poor manager behaved or treated the team members. I definitely remember thinking, *I'll never do* that *to people.*

"Now, you may not know *what to do* necessarily, but the worse the managers you have are, the more it builds this narrow path for you to walk down."

Right. Exactly. Thus you see more employee turnover in areas where these bad managers work. It is the number-one reason employees leave their jobs.

During my time as a Dale Carnegie franchise owner, I joined an organization that served as an executive mentoring board to me and nine other small business owners. We became the board of directors for each other. We met together with a business coach once a month. Each month, we would present the business issues that each of us were working on. We were each accountable to this board.

"Was this a Vistage-type organization, a peer-to-peer advisory organization for executives of small to mid-size businesses?"

Yes, although mine was called "The Alternative Board" (TAB). It really helped me. Their support gave me the *attaboys* I needed, and I could run ideas past them. They would tell me when they thought my ideas would likely fail or if they believed they might not be accepted, once they were out in the open. I saved myself some mistakes.

I enjoyed that. I also appreciated having people around who believed in me and would give me honest feedback—without politics.

If you are going to own your own business, or if you're going to be a CEO, you're not going to get honest feedback. If you had that in the past as a manager, and it feeds you, it is important to seek out a place where you can get that kind of feedback.

> **If you are going to own your own business, or if you're going to be a CEO, you're not going to get honest feedback.**

Not everybody needs it, but I think women do. We like feedback. The good news is, there are good resources out there to help.

Lieutenant General Kathleen M. Gainey
U.S. Army, Retired

Lt. Gen. Kathy Gainey had this to say about her own self-development process:

> After I was a platoon leader, I had the opportunity to go to staff, which means I accepted an administrative role after serving in command in the field.
>
> One day, the battalion commander called me in and said, "I'm thinking of having you to go into the Assistant S1, or the Assistant S2 or S3 position. What do you think about that?"
>
> I said, "Well, sure, but let me think about that."
>
> I probably should not have said that, but I did not know what all that meant, at first. So, I went and talked to people who were in those jobs. They said, "Okay. Here's what you would be doing. This is what I've learned from that job."
>
> Then, I went back and talked to the battalion commander and our senior NCO, First Sergeant Lutrell. They both said, "Assistant S2/3. This is a good job. Go for that. That's going to help you understand different things."

And you do! When you are down below on the career ladder, you are thinking the people up above have no clue what is going on. Yet, here they are, giving you guidance. Meanwhile, you are thinking, *They're asleep. They don't really know.*

But when you get up there, you realize, *Oh! Here are the challenges they were faced with.*

> **When you are down below on the career ladder, you are thinking the people up above have no clue what is going on. But when you get up there, you realize, *Oh! Here are the challenges they were faced with.***

That is why the guidance that was being given to us down below may have seemed spotty, because it was spotty. They did not have all the information. But they were trying to shape the opportunity for the unit to succeed.

I interjected, "So there was somebody kind of watching out for you, or at least advising you. You didn't have to figure it all out on your own."

Absolutely. I always had people coaching and mentoring me or pushing me. And of course, I had my dad, who was in the military. I would always talk to my dad.

Now, back then, I was not making phone calls. It was all handwritten letters. But they would always be encouraging me.

"In the situations where you would then take the job you were unfamiliar with, were you reading everything you could in order to learn on the job, or were you asking people for help?"

Both. I often had to go and learn, read books, and read regulations, because my boss did not have time to teach all that. He had his own job to do. He

> **I often had to go and learn...because my boss did not have time to teach all that. He had his own job to do.**

would just say, "Here's your mission. Here's your task."

"Okay. But what regulation do I go to?"

"Go ask *them*."

So, I would sit with the NCOs or the Army civilians (or whoever) and they would show me what to do and how to do it. They would show me the regulations so that I could learn it.

That was one thing my dad advised: "Always read the regulation to know what's *supposed* to happen."

If you do not read the regulation, or the standard operating procedure, you will never know if you're doing it the way it's *supposed* to be done, or if you're doing it differently. If you are doing it differently, you need to know why. Otherwise, you are just taking a shortcut, perhaps.

I shared this in response: "I have observed women who are afraid to step outside their comfort level without *first* going back to school, without *first* getting trained. Their natural reaction is, 'Well, first let me get trained up on that.' Then they complain when someone else, usually a guy, just steps forward to volunteer and gets the job."

You must sometimes make your own opportunities by going into those jobs that you do not feel comfortable in. But you should not hesitate to ask questions. Do not hesitate to take time at night to do your own research. Do your own learning. Then, come back the next day and say, "I read this last night, yet I know that we're doing it this way. Why are we doing it this way?"

You must sometimes make your own opportunities by going into those jobs that you do not feel comfortable in.

Then have them explain it. Sometimes they would say to me, "What do you mean, 'We're doing it differently'?"

I would say, "Well, here's the regulation," or, "Here's the manual that says how we're supposed to do this and we're not doing it that way. We are doing it this way and here are the key differences. Why are we doing it this way?"

Sometimes they do not realize themselves that they are not doing it in accordance with the instructions. So, then they start thinking, *Oh! Here is a person who is adding value. This person is helping us to make sure we are doing it correctly, so we're not making mistakes or deviating from the requirement.*

I asked, "When you would go and ask questions, who were the *thems* you were asking?"

Sometimes it was a peer. Sometimes it was an officer senior to me. Sometimes it was a subordinate who was teaching me, like our noncommissioned officers.

Sometimes they would say, "Well, that's a good question. I don't know why we're doing it that way."

They would help me go find out if there was some situation that had caused us to change and we just never changed back. Or we might discover that people had just started doing it by rote memory and maybe that fell apart. Or maybe people just took somebody's word for how to do it, when they did not know how it should have been done, either.

That is why I would go back to review the regulation. That is how I learned.

REFLECTIONS:

Life is a self-development journey. Every day brings new opportunities to discover things we never knew before. It gives us yet another chance to look at old things in new ways, provided we are inquisitive and keep an open mind.

The most effective leaders have a self-development mindset. Rather than fearing they do not have all the answers, they are never afraid to ask questions. In fact, they continuously seek to gain greater understanding by more asking questions. They know that asking great questions can help solve problems, build bridges, foster creativity, and drive innovation.

Never lack faith in yourself just because you do not have all the answers. Accept the fact that you will never have all the answers, even if you go back to school to get yet another degree. Simply surround yourself with smart people. Take advantage of learning from them and do your own research in your own time.

Granted, there are some career paths that require a license and/or an advanced degree to practice the trade, or some number of hours of continuing education every year. If that kind of role is your objective, then of course, get the required education.

Accept the fact that you will never have all the answers, even if you go back to school to get yet another degree. Simply surround yourself with smart people.

But in general, you will be amazed at the doors that will open to you if you simply strive to creatively broaden your knowledge base, build on your awareness of the world, and expand the base of your professional contacts.

As part of your annual professional development plan, attend seminars; volunteer with charitable organizations or the arts; participate in programs offered by your city, your industry association, or professional women's organizations; or get involved in other things that pique your interest. You never know where these opportunities might take you.

The important thing is to keep learning and growing. Never let a lack of education stop you from doing what you really want to do in life. Believe in yourself, remain determined, and learn as you go.

By doing so, you just might get to the C-suite faster than you ever imagined.

INTROSPECTIONS:

1   When was the last time you just went away by yourself
     and were quiet? When do you just sit still long enough to
     really listen to your heart?

2   Do you ever deliberately take time out to reflect and
     evaluate the areas in which you would like to improve
     your skills and breadth of knowledge? If so, what is your
     process? If not, then plan to do so.

3   What kinds of things do you take advantage of to keep
     learning—to give yourself that WOW factor?

4   What has proven so beneficial, in terms of your own
     self-development, that you would recommend it to others
     coming up the ladder behind you?

TWELVE

Victimhood

Be open to hearing what is said, and then think about it—even if it seems completely unfair or completely off the mark, or totally crazy, think about it. There's probably some grain of truth in what's being said.

-KERRY HEALEY, PHD
Inaugural President, Milken Center for Advancing the American Dream

Having led a leadership development program for high-potential women, I cannot begin to count the number of women I have known to play the victim card upon losing a promotional opportunity. Victimhood is a somewhat common trait that otherwise high-potential individuals must overcome if they are ever going to achieve the level of performance their superiors believe they are capable of.

According to the *Cambridge Dictionary*, victimhood is "the condition of having been hurt, damaged, or made to suffer, especially when you want people to feel sorry for you, or to use it as an excuse for something."

Most everyone knows that losing hurts, especially when the loss is highly visible. A high-visibility loss, like losing a big promotion, can trigger disappointment, embarrassment, anger, an impulse to publicly blame others, and a feeling of victimhood. No one wants to be viewed as a loser.

Yet, from every loss can spring new opportunity. We have the chance to learn, strengthen our skills, and build tighter bonds with our stakeholders. By **By displaying the best side of ourselves after a loss, we stand to garner even greater support.** leveraging a loss as an opportunity to learn and grow, we increase our likelihood to win next time. We have a wonderful opportunity to serve as an inspirational role model to others. By displaying the best side of ourselves after a loss, we stand to garner even greater support.

Face it. You serve as a role model in everything you do. Someone is always watching you, assessing you, and—for better or worse—learning from you. Don't you want others to be impressed and proud of you, regardless of whether you win or lose? For this reason alone, it is important to consider the kind of role model you want to be, especially when you end up losing.

Being a stellar role model, and not playing the victim, is about demonstrating good sportsmanship, humility, a dedication to self-improvement, and a commitment to building stronger relationships. It is about striving to be the best you can be, no matter the outcome. It is about *not* making excuses or blaming others.

Playing the victim will hold you back. It will not help you get into the C-suite.

People who are self-aware problem-solvers, who accept responsibility for failure and proactively take corrective action after a loss, are the ones who are most likely to win the next time and who ultimately rise to the top.

> **Playing the victim will hold you back. It will not help you get into the C-suite.**

Becoming such a person requires an inward focus. While it is good to appreciate whatever it is that your peers do exceptionally well, and it is valuable to understand the reasons why those who get promoted do, one must be careful about focusing too much on other people. Do not compare yourself to others. Do not get into a competitive, self-critical trap.

Of course, there are fewer slots the higher up you go on the career ladder. Realistically, there will always be competition for the next step on the ladder—unless you are creative enough to create your own next role. There are always different variables that go into any hiring decision. There are always different reasons why a particular individual may be awarded a position you want. Hiring and promotional decisions are often out of your control. So, focus on what you can control: your attitude, your behavior, and your own performance.

> **Focus on what you can control: your attitude, your behavior, and your own performance.**

"What Can I Learn from This Loss?"

When you fail to win a promotion that you thought you should have been granted, ask yourself, *What part of this do I own? Did I not articulate my value in a meaningful way? Did I not raise my hand to take that risky assignment because I thought I did not check every box for it? What part of this loss do I just need to let go? What can I learn from this?*

If you believe someone you may be competing with does something particularly well, make a study of that. Learn from them. Proactively invite them to coffee or lunch. Sit down with them and say, "I so admire the way you do these things. Can you tell me more about that?"

If over time you are doing everything you can do that is within your control, and you are confident that you are performing well in your job, yet you are not getting the promotional opportunities you believe you deserve, then pick up your toys and go elsewhere. Do not waste your time playing a game you simply cannot win. I personally learned that the hard way.

As a corporate leader, I have always believed it is important for team members to understand what they need to do to get promoted. It is also important for them to understand why they may have been passed over for a promotion. People deserve to be supported with constructive feedback throughout the process. I never wanted anyone on my team to be blindsided.

Why more managers do not do this for their team members, to help them develop, I do not know. But anyone who desires a role in senior leadership needs to figure it out. You cannot always rely on others to proactively tell you why you may have been passed over. You need to be proactive and ask.

> **You cannot always rely on others to proactively tell you why you may have been passed over. You need to be proactive and ask.**

Finding out why you have been passed over for a promotion is somewhat akin to holding a loss review, just as good sales teams do to improve their probability of winning in the future. If you are not familiar with the loss review concept, I will share this story about a female sales rep, Kathryn, whom I worked with at AT&T several years ago. Kathryn impressed me so much by her after-loss actions, I have never forgotten her, nor the valuable lesson she taught me.

Kathryn managed some of AT&T's largest national accounts. When I first met her, she had been steadfastly working for months to close a multimillion-dollar deal with one of her accounts. She had a huge commission riding on it, and all sales management eyes were on her. You can imagine the shock and angst when she lost that deal.

The thing that impressed me most about her was that when things did not work out the way she had expected, she never lost her composure. She did not blame her engineering support team for not being service-oriented enough. She did not blame the management team for not being flexible enough. She did not blame the customer for making a bad decision. She did not blame the winning competitor for undercutting our price or for being sneaky.

Instead, she focused on upping her game. She went straight to work building even stronger relationships with the client's key decision-makers and influencers. She became more determined than ever to become the very best, most dependable, solutions-oriented, WOW factor provider in the business.

With a smile on her face and an *I have confidence in me* attitude, she scheduled one-on-one loss review meetings with every individual involved in the client's decision-making process. She did what she probably should have done in the first place to fully understand the client's decision-making process, along with everyone's underlying needs, priorities, and expectations.

With great humility, she asked each of the stakeholders to share in detail, from their own perspectives, what we did or did not do that caused us to lose the deal. More importantly, she accepted and acknowledged where, when, and how she had failed to meet their expectations and what we, as a team, needed to improve going forward. Then, she kept in contact with every key stakeholder, on a regular basis.

> **She accepted and acknowledged where, when, and how she had failed to meet their expectations and what we, as a team, needed to improve going forward.**

Her sales manager told her she was wasting her time, now that the big money was off the table. But she was determined. Meanwhile, the winning competitor began implementing their multi-campus solution. Whenever a problem occurred that was not immediately addressed by our competitor, Kathryn would be the first one in the door to fully understand the issue and to suggest an alternative approach, no matter how trivial.

It was not long into the implementation process when our competitor had a significant problem. Our competitor had no alternative but to delay the cut-over schedule. The customer was not happy. Because Kathryn had remained at the customer's beck and call, some of the stakeholders made sure Kathryn became aware of every problem. Rather than disparaging them, Kathryn volunteered our own systems engineers to troubleshoot and advise on workarounds, which saved the day for both the customer and our competitor.

Whenever additional problems came up, Kathryn was always there to volunteer advice, pro bono. At every step, she proved our value and further solidified her relationship with the customer executives. At some point, the customer asked her for a proposal for the remaining, not-yet installed nodes. To make a long story short, we eventually won all the business back.

If it had not been for Kathryn's humble determination to hold loss review meetings with everyone involved in the client's decision-making process, ensuring that she understood their full set of expectations and what we could do to improve our performance, Kathryn never would have won back all that business.

For me, that was an incredible learning experience. Much of my own success throughout my career stemmed from Kathryn's role-model behavior. More importantly, I learned from her how important it is to go through that process *before* decisions are made, to be best positioned to win.

While interviewing our now-familiar women on top, I was anxious to hear what they have observed along these lines and if they had any suggestions for women to improve their chances when it comes to promotional opportunities.

Melissa Reiff
Former Chairwoman and CEO
The Container Store

During my conversation with Melissa Reiff, I said to her, "I routinely hear some women say, 'I am so capable. I could do this job. But *he* got the job. *He's* not nearly as experienced or as capable as I am.' What would you say to those women who are watching guys get promoted but they're not?"

I would say, "It's wrong and it makes me crazy."

If I were them, I would make my dissatisfaction known and then I would look for another opportunity in another company that values me.

Unfortunately, this happens more often than it should. I hope it is getting better and it is happening less, and less, and less.

I agree.

It makes me crazy, as well, when someone who is clearly less capable is selected for promotion over a far more capable person who clearly conveyed their promotional desires and career objectives to the hiring manager and key influencers. If this happens to you, don't hesitate to ask those in the know why you were passed over. There may be a perfectly valid reason.

It also makes me crazy when someone expects a promotion, but they don't ask for the job. If this applies to you, ask yourself what you need to do differently. Make your career objectives known to higher-ups. Get some coaching if need be, so you can confidently ask for the job you want next time.

If you are doing all the right things and you are still passed over for promotion, be honest with yourself. Are you in a no-win situation? If the proverbial handwriting is on the wall, then move on. As Melissa suggested, make your dissatisfaction known and look for an opportunity in an organization where the culture offers a better fit and there is greater potential for upward mobility. Life is too short to stay where you are not appreciated or rewarded fairly. Refuse to be a victim.

Nancy Howell Agee
President and CEO
Carilion Clinic

During my conversation with Nancy Agee, president and CEO of Carilion Clinic, I mentioned to her, "I have heard from countless women who apparently think that if they do a really good job, somebody is going to magically recognize that. It is as though they believe if they rack up a bunch of little gold stars on their paper, then they will get promoted. They are dumbfounded when there is an opening and, *voilà*, someone else gets the job. What do you suggest women should do when that happens?"

Let us talk about interviews—when people are looking for another job and they are interviewing. My recommendation is to *practice*.
- Practice lowering your voice.
- Practice being both slow and modulating, as well as creating energy.

Know there is a balance there. You need to practice all that with someone. We practice that here. I mean we practice, practice, and practice. It gives you the confidence you need.

Plan for multiple questions and an answer, but not a scripted answer. How would you share something about what you have done? How would you describe that?

I have interviewed countless women. Too often, I find them nervous. Their voice gets more high-pitched. They start shaking their legs.

Do not cross your legs. Sit up straight. You are in an interview. And finally, dress for the job you want to have, not the job you have.

I then asked her, "Do you think dressing appropriately is an issue that has always been a problem, or do you believe this issue is getting worse over time?"

It's interesting. I do not know if it is getting worse, but it is something I have seen.

You have got to be so careful. If you are going to wear a skirt, you want to be sure that it does not hike up when you sit down. Women do have practical concerns that you've got to think through when you're interviewing.

Another thing I have found is that women are often apologetic for expressing their value. It comes through in several ways. For example, they will say, "This really doesn't sound like much, but..."

Don't use the word *but*. This *but*... That *but*... Stop that! You need to present yourself as though you have the confidence to do the job.

> **You need to present yourself as though you have the confidence to do the job.**

I just said this to a woman I think the world of. She's so bright and so capable. She was in my office, and we were chatting about something. The third time I heard her say, "I'm really sorry to say this, but..." I said, "Okay. Level set here. Do not apologize for your opinions."

She said, "What? I don't think I do that."

"Let me just parrot back what I heard."

"Oh. I guess I say that all the time."

"Yes, and it's hurting your credibility."

Even very confident women—physicians—do that.

I appreciate you writing a book about this because I think there are some very practical things that women do not even think about in terms of how they are presenting themselves. Face it, men can have the same issues, but they somehow do not get the attention.

Those are just some practical things that I think women can do. They often are just as, or even more, capable than men. It's the classic Ginger Rogers, dancing backwards in high heels.

But you have got to get rid of the high-pitched voice that is not modulated when asked for your opinion.

To that, I replied, "I have found some women executives are not even comfortable talking about this. It is interesting to hear you say that you see this in women doctors. Most people think of doctors as being so professional and highly educated. We assume doctors must be very competent."

In some ways. But when you get people out of their comfort level, even though they may be very competent with a patient interaction, for instance—and you can draw the same parallel to other industries—when you put them in a boardroom or with other colleagues, or with people in other disciplines, you will see their confidence shut down.

I have another colleague who is so smart and so capable. Yet, she uses phrases like, "Take a deep breath. Take a deep breath. Okay. I'm just going to say this..." or, "I know I don't know much about this, but..."

The fact is, we want to hear her opinion. We believe she *does* know what she is talking about. But I guess she must color it to make herself feel comfortable.

I said to her, just last week, "Do you hear yourself? Do you know how you are undoing the good that you bring, by coloring it first, as if you don't have a reason to have that opinion?"

> **Do you know how you are undoing the good that you bring, by coloring it first, as if you don't have a reason to have that opinion?**

It frustrates me that women do that to themselves.

When I interjected, "I wonder where we pick that up," Nancy replied,

Good question.

I then changed the subject a bit and said, "Some people become victims because they are afraid to go over their manager's head to let the leader above them know the manager is a problem and is causing issues for the organization. What would you say about that?"

I think when you can put your insights forward as being for the good of the organization—not for yourself—and try to be constructive, that is totally different from being a complainer.

Kerry Healey
Inaugural President
Milken Center for Advancing the American Dream

When I spoke with Kerry Healey, PhD, a former lieutenant governor and university president, I asked, "What would you suggest women should do when they lose a promotional opportunity to someone else?"

I'd suggest that they go, humbly, to whomever made that decision and ask them for feedback. They should be open to hearing what is said, and then think about it—even if it seems completely unfair or completely off the mark, or totally crazy, think about it. There's probably some grain of truth in what's being said.

On occasion, you need to think about your weaknesses. As a leader, always take responsibility for a failure, whether it is really your fault or not. As a practice, take responsibility for failure, just because it relieves everyone else of the responsibility and ends controversy. Then you can move forward.

> As a leader, always take responsibility for a failure, whether it is really your fault or not.

I would suggest that people think about what other people say about them, and what kind of advice people give to them. Seek constructive feedback from someone who really knows how you are perceived. Spend some time thinking about it, without being defensive, without trying to rebut it. Just let it sink in for a long time and think about it. You're likely to learn something.

Wendy Johnson
Former President and CEO
Dale Carnegie franchise, Atlanta, GA

When I spoke with Wendy Johnson, I mentioned, "It's amazing how many women think they are doing such a great job that they should automatically get promoted. Yet, when the promotion does not happen, they come to me saying, 'I don't know why David got that promotion and I didn't.'"

Some people think that they will get promoted based on time in position. A lot of people think that just because they have been there the longest, they deserve to be promoted.

I had a similar situation with two administrative people who worked for me. I simply had to bring each of them into my office to tell them, point-blank, "I can't promote you and I can't pay you any more than I currently do. I have got to be honest with you. If you want to make more money and you want to have a different position, it is not going to happen here."

I then explained, "Every year you come to me hoping you'll get a raise of some kind. But I must be honest. I value you, but you are at the top of the pay scale. I cannot afford to pay you any more than you are making. I understand if you have to leave."

They stayed. They liked their position enough to forgo the future increases. But that is not always the case.

Most managers will not address those things out of fear of losing them. Instead, managers think to themselves, *Oh, I hope she doesn't ask. I hope she doesn't ask because then I'll have to tell her.* They avoid those conversations.

So, you need to find out what the reality of your work environment is. If you want more money than you are currently earning, but there is no room for you to get a raise or promotion where you are, you need to know this. If you are not sure you are in the right position, you should know about an assessment called the *Strong Interest Inventory* career test.

The *Strong Interest Inventory* identifies what you are best at, what environment makes you happy, what environments you thrive in, what environments are the worst for you. It helps you identify what drives you.

Sometimes you do not like your job because you are doing something you are not well suited for. You might discover, through this test, that you really should be doing something else. That something else could mean upward movement potential.

> **Sometimes you do not like your job because you are doing something you are not well suited for.**

I think that you need to do a little introspection when you get stuck. There are a lot of resources out there to help—many times, even within your own company. You need to ask.

Lieutenant General Kathleen M. Gainey
U.S. Army, Retired

I asked Lt. Gen. Kathy Gainey, "Why do you think some women say, 'I do not understand why these guys are getting promoted. They are doing the same job I am doing. I know I am doing a far better job, yet *they* get the promotion'?"

The great thing about her response is that it highlights the dual advantage of developing other people—not only do *they* win because their skills improve, *you* also win because you're then freed up to do the sorts of higher-level tasks that get you promoted.

> I think sometimes we tend to do the things that we are comfortable with, and we do the things that we know need to be done. But we should be empowering others to do those things, instead.

> One of the key things that somebody taught me was, "Do only what *you* have to do. If there are other tasks, just because you know how to do it, and you're good at it, doesn't mean you *should* be doing it."

Develop the skill in someone else and teach them that skill by getting them to do it. Help them learn a new skill. Empower them. Free yourself up to do the things that only you can do, which is walking around, creating relationships, checking on things, understanding how much progress people have made on projects, and motivating people.

That other person can't do those things. They cannot keep a pulse on all the things going on. But you can, by walking around. You can, by motivating people as you talk to them and empower them.

> **Free yourself up to do the things that only you can do, which is walking around, creating relationships, checking on things, understanding how much progress people have made on projects, and motivating people.**

I think maybe people do not get promoted because they do not avail themselves of the opportunity to do these things: walk around, talk to people, motivate them. Instead, they are doing the day-to-day minutiae rather than letting someone else do that. They could be teaching those people another skill and building their confidence.

So, the senior leaders do not see them as ready to handle more complex tasks because they are not developing relationships with others, they are not empowering people, or they are not getting above the day-to-day fray.

I asked, "Are there other things one can do when they find out someone else got the promotion they thought they deserved?"

I would often say to myself, *What is it they're good at that I'm not? Maybe that was a skill that was critical, that was needed. Maybe I need to sharpen that skill.*

Or, *What is it that they are able to shape, that I can't shape, because I don't have that skill, or I don't have that talent?*

Or, *Maybe that job needed more financial management*, which is a big weakness of mine. *Maybe it's a skill I need to develop*, whether it was an interpersonal or a technical skill.

"Was there ever a time in your career when you really wanted a particular job, but you didn't get it?"

Oh, lots of times! But as time goes on, you find yourself in an even better job. I would never look back and say, "Gee. I wish I'd gotten that other job."

"Did you ever think to yourself, *I did not get that other job because of X; I am going to shore up that skill and make sure I get that job next time*?"

I would just say to myself, *Okay. What was that skill that I might have been lacking, that they got selected for?* I would try to make myself competitive for the next opportunity.

REFLECTIONS:

In the workplace and beyond, some women elect to play the victim when things do not go their way. But blaming others for one's loss and being resentful or jealous of another's success is not the way to get ahead. In fact, such displays almost guarantee otherwise. You only hurt yourself.

While we may be granted our first promotion or two seemingly out of the blue, do not expect that to continue as you go up the ladder. When we expect others to automatically appreciate and reward us for crossing every "T" and dotting every "I," we set ourselves up for victimhood.

Do not blame the winner, and do not make excuses for yourself.

Many promotional decisions are beyond our control. There could be any number of reasons why one person is promoted over another. So do not blame the winner, and do not make excuses for yourself. Instead, ask for developmental opportunities for yourself and give developmental opportunities to those below you. Meanwhile, let those above you know your interests and intentions. Practice being the best role-model leader you can be.

If you are aiming for executive leadership, be responsible for managing your own career. Whenever someone else wins a promotion, be gracious and congratulate them. Learn from them and prepare yourself to move on to bigger and better things. And yes, if you must, move on to a different organization where your contributions will be valued. Life is too short to be resentful.

Good things happen to those who are proactive and hold themselves accountable. That is one of the keys to executive leadership.

INTROSPECTIONS:

1 Have you ever seen someone play the victim card when someone else won a promotion? If so, did you feel sorry for the one who lost or was it obvious to you why they might have been passed over?

2 Think about the last time you did not win a promotion that you had hoped for or expected.
   a. How did you react when you learned someone else had won the position? Did you play the victim?
   b. What, if anything, could you have done to better prepare to win that promotion?
   c. What can you do to better prepare for promotion going forward?

3 If you are a manager, what can you do to better prepare your team members for promotional opportunities?

Words of Wisdom

Get out of your comfort level. Read. Make
friends with people who are not like you.
-NANCY HOWELL AGEE
President and CEO, Carilion Clinic

A s I concluded each interview with our now-so-familiar women on top, I asked each to share their final thoughts in the form of advice for three groups of women: those in high school, those in college, and those now pursuing careers. The point was to have them summarize a few key takeaways—silver bullets— to kickstart and streamline the next phase of your journey to executive leadership.

I hope that by the end of this chapter, you will have come to understand—from these authentically down-to-earth executives, from different backgrounds, with different educational experiences, who followed vastly different career paths, and leveraged their own unique strengths within an assortment of industries—there is no one perfect career plan or leadership style that will take you to the top. You simply follow the unique path that works best for you.

Likewise, there is no single most effective way to lead. There is no one best company or ideal industry. Thankfully, the world is full of magnificent alternatives, just as the world is full of amazing women with their own special gifts to offer to the world.

> **The world is full of magnificent alternatives, just as the world is full of amazing women with their own special gifts to offer to the world.**

Before I present the key takeaways from our women on top, I am going to address a great question that was asked of me recently, one I did not ask our women on top but perhaps should have:

> If you had to sum up your personal leadership philosophy in just four words, what would those four words be?

My four words would be these: *Learn, Love, Laugh,* and *Brave.*

Much of what we have covered throughout this book has essentially been about these four words. These words have served as the guiding stars throughout my own career. They are also foundational to any advice I would give to any career-minded woman, whether she is at the beginning of or well down the path along her leadership journey.

This is what these four foundational words mean to me.

Learn: Your entire life is a learning experience. Be a lifelong learner. Never stop being curious. Never hesitate to ask questions. The smartest, most knowledgeable, and perceptive leaders I know are incredibly inquisitive. Be open to new perspectives. Never take anything at face value. Strive to uncover the truth—there is always more to every story. Assess *why* things are the way they are. If needed information is not forthcoming, dig deeper. When you misfire, assess what the experience has taught you and grow from any newfound knowledge. When given an opportunity to try something new, take it and learn from it.

> When given an opportunity to try something new, take it and learn from it.

Love: Do what you love and love what you do—life is too short to do otherwise. Doing what you love will give you energy—your work will be a joy, and the hours will fly by. Encourage those around you to do what they love, so your team can achieve WOW factor results. Delegate those things you do not love to do to someone who does love to do such things—they can leverage their strengths and grow their skills while doing so. Seek to love something about everyone, even if they do not seem loveable—you just might change their life as well as your own.

Laugh: Love and laughter are two of life's greatest gifts. Be self-aware enough to laugh at yourself—never take yourself too seriously. If you make a mistake, laugh about it. Laughter dispels self-doubt and self-pity and allows you to move on to bigger and better things. It also dispels anxiety, resentment, and fear—it is a sign of mental toughness and resilience. Laughter is restorative—it can lighten the heaviness of the most difficult situations. It reinforces social bonds and improves both our mental and physical health. Attitude is everything, so pick a good one and let laughter set your spirit free.

Attitude is everything, so pick a good one and let laughter set your spirit free.

Brave: Fear is a natural reaction, but courage is a choice. True leaders choose to be brave even though they may be scared. When given the opportunity to take on a challenge beyond your comfort zone, do it—you just might impress the heck out of yourself, and you will serve as a role model to anyone who doubted you. Being brave allows you to live without regrets. Rather than looking back at the end of your life and wishing *if only*, be brave enough to learn, love, and laugh about having done them. Never be afraid to do what is right. Stand for the truth and grow your leadership skills. If you want to be in the C-suite, you must choose to be brave.

Now, here is my own advice to women at various points along their career paths.

First, for young women in high school:
1. Do you have a calling? Is there something you just know in your heart that you really want to do with your life? If so, learn everything about it that you can *well before you decide whether to go to college.* Talk to as many people as you can who have that career and ask them for their advice. Listen to what they say, evaluate your resources, and if you still

want to pursue that career, then prepare an action plan and
go for it.

2. If you are not sure what to do with your life, then take the
opportunity to interview business, military, and government
leaders whenever you can. Whether they are family
members, the parents of your friends, friends of your
parents, your doctor, or professionals in the places where
your family does business, what you can learn in a
30-minute chat could prove invaluable. Ask these people
how they got where they are and what they studied in
college. Ask them for any suggestions they may have for you.
It will be a great way to get comfortable stepping beyond
your comfort zone.

3. Learn to be a good follower as well as a leader. Participate in
and volunteer for leadership positions in extracurricular
activities.

4. Get a part-time job to earn your own spending money. This
will not only teach you self-reliance and financial
management, but it will also provide you with insights into
operating a business.

Next, for college women:

1. Participate in and volunteer for leadership positions within
on-campus and community-based activities to broaden your
awareness about life and leadership.

2. Take the initiative to pay for at least a portion of your tuition
and living expenses on your own. This will help you learn to
make sound financial decisions.

3. Conduct informational interviews with business, military, and government leaders located near campus. In a 30-minute meeting, ask about their organizational objectives, the benefits they deliver to their target markets, and the types of positions appropriate to college students and new grads who have your educational background. Not only will these interviews help you step beyond your comfort zone, but you may also discover career options you may not yet be aware of.

Finally, for career women who may be feeling stuck:
Never underestimate the value of informational interviews outside of your current industry and/or functional career path.
Informational interviews are not about seeking a job. The intent of these 45-minute meetings is for you to learn more about different work environments that you might find intriguing and where you might excel. To obtain an informational interview where you have no existing contacts, look to LinkedIn. Ask your connections to introduce you to a leader of an organization on your "intrigue" list, whom they are connected to and whom they know well. Make the most of each meeting by exploring the ins and outs of that industry beforehand and whether there might be a fit somewhere for someone with your unique strengths and background. This will help you assess your value beyond your current capacity.

Whatever your stage of life, my wish for you is that you will never miss an opportunity to share the best of who you are, wherever you go.

Now it is time to hear the final thoughts that our amazing women on top have for you.

Melissa Reiff
Former Chairwoman and CEO
The Container Store

When I asked Melissa Reiff, "What advice do you have for the next generation, for those leaving high school or college?" she had this to say:

Well, you've got to get an education. I believe it's important to have a college degree, for a myriad of reasons.

I would counsel a high schooler to reach out to as many people as you can—your parents' friends, whoever—and just request 15 or 20 minutes of their time to ask them some questions about their experiences. Think about the questions you could ask that can help you determine, as best as possible, what kinds of things might interest you. What floats your boat? What might you be passionate about? What might give you a bit of a spark?

All this is important to consider, because college is getting more and more expensive. You want to ensure that you are spending your time and money wisely.

Then, I would tell that high school graduate, "College is fun." I certainly had my fun. Try to make sure that you keep everything in balance as you are going through those four or five years, in terms of being responsible.

And remember, it's a new world in terms of social media. Be smart. Be careful. Be wise about that.

It's a new world in terms of social media. Be smart. Be careful. Be wise about that. In those four years in college, from that very first freshman year, look for opportunities to reach out to people in different careers. People do want to help young people, but realize their lives are busy. We only have twenty-four hours in a day. But look for those opportunities to reach out and ask questions.

And look for opportunities to be involved. That is important. Do an internship in college if you can. Internships are so beneficial for so many reasons: exposure, networking, experience in a *real* environment.

I finally asked Melissa, "What advice do you have for those women leaving college?"

Well, for the most part, all I just said applies to women after college. It never stops.

It is always important to continue to be inquisitive, curious, take initiative, and look for those opportunities. And, following college, be more aggressive in networking with companies. Understand all the different industries and opportunities available.

I sit on the executive board at the Cox School of Business at Southern Methodist University (SMU). They do an amazing job helping students to network and prepare for their careers.

I recently visited with a smart, articulate young woman. She graduated from Texas A&M. She's been in the workforce for four years, married three years, and in that phase of her life where she is asking herself, *What is my next step? Do I like what I am doing now? What do I really want to do? What else is out there?*

It is always important to continue to be inquisitive, curious, take initiative, and look for those opportunities.

What if you're one of those people who just doesn't have a clear vision of "I want to be a doctor" or "I want to be a lawyer" or "I want to be in the oil industry" or "I want to be this or that," but you're very much a people person, smart and articulate?

The world is your oyster, as they say. But, on the other hand, it can be daunting. You have to work through it. Be determined and persevere.

The world is your oyster, as they say. But, on the other hand, it can be daunting. You have to work through it. Be determined and persevere.

And good luck to you. I love to see women get ahead.

Jodi Berg
President and CEO
Vita-Mix Corporation

I asked Jodi Berg, PhD, "What advice do you have for the next generation? You have two daughters, so you've probably gone through this, but how would you advise girls leaving high school, young women leaving college, and women who may feel like they're stuck in their careers?"

Probably the most important advice—and it would relate to all three groups—is, if I could wave my magic WOW wand, I would want to help women of every age truly believe in their heart of hearts that *they matter.*

Let me make this personal. As a human being, you matter. Because of the person you are, and because of the experiences you have been through—whatever those experiences might be—you are *unique.*

Conscientiously create your "I want to be like that" bucket and get rid of all the negative stuff that you have been told.

Conscientiously create your "I want to be like that" bucket and get rid of all the negative stuff that you have been told.

Then, because of who you are, identify what you are uniquely positioned to do that is going to make a difference. Having a positive impact on others is the wind beneath our wings.

In full transparency, even my own two daughters are still not to a point where they truly understand their value. Ladies, the value is in us already!

I want women to realize that they do not have to walk into a room and think that everyone else in the room is smarter than they are.

Women should be able to walk into that room and say, "WOW. We are all smart; we all matter; and there's something of value that we all can add," not for the sake of talking, not for the sake of being recognized, not for the sake of taking up air or real estate in the room, but for the sake of this symbiotic exchange of value.

Recognize that everyone else has value and so do you. It is because we both have value that we can become better together.

Nancy Howell Agee
President and CEO
Carilion Clinic

I asked Nancy Agee, president and CEO of Carilion Clinic, "What do you have to say to young women leaving high school, those leaving college, and to that woman who is mid-career and maybe feels stuck?"

For the high school students: Get out of your comfort level. Read. Make friends with people who are not like you.

For the college students and graduates: Understand that you are not finishing your education. You are just beginning. Be curious.

Really for all three, but especially for the woman who is anxious to move on or move up, here is something that I did early on: I got involved in a couple of organizations. It's the quintessential *lean in.* Raise your hand. Take on new challenges. Take on new opportunities.

You are not finishing your education. You are just beginning. Be curious.

Linda Rutherford
Senior Vice President, Chief Communications Officer
Southwest Airlines

I asked Linda Rutherford, "What advice do you have for young women who are leaving high school, women leaving college, and women who are in their careers, but feeling a little bit stuck?"

Today, my advice to those leaving high school is to be invested in a college education.

If you are going to advance, if you are going to build personal wealth, if you are going to live a broader life, you have got to get a college education. I would highly encourage anyone who's leaving high school to consider that path. I know it isn't for everyone. It may not be possible for everyone, but I would still highly encourage that exploration.

To someone leaving college, I would say to remember that your first job is not a life sentence. From it, you will learn the things that you really enjoy doing. You will potentially learn some things that you will find you absolutely do not want to spend your life doing. I do think that college graduates put a lot of pressure on themselves to make that first role that perfect role. It just may not be.

For women trying to get that next promotion, I go back to, know who you are and share who you are.

To someone leaving college, I would say to remember that your first job is not a life sentence.

Understand all those strengths that you bring to the table. Some call it "articulating your value." I call it "know your brand."

Be able to share with others how you're going to be able to contribute to the success of the team and to the success of the company. Then you, in turn, will be successful as a result.

Kerry Healey
Inaugural President
Milken Center for Advancing the American Dream

I asked Kerry Healey, PhD, "What advice do you have for the next generation?"

To those leaving high school, I would suggest that they study very broadly. They should go into college with an open mind and not necessarily think that they are going to focus on only one thing. Plan to take courses across a lot of different areas that challenge them and open their eyes to new perspectives, history, and new parts of the world.

People going into college should live abroad. They should do the international exchange student experience, at least once, if not twice. They should probably take as many opportunities to learn different cultures as they possibly can.

I would strongly urge them, also, to get serious about becoming proficient in the language that they were studying in high school. Make sure that they can live and do business in another culture, and in another language, fluently. That is incredibly important and something that Americans do not do enough. That would be one.

> **Make sure that they can live and do business in another culture, and in another language, fluently. That is incredibly important and something that Americans do not do enough.**

For people just graduating from college, I would recommend that they work very hard and take as many opportunities as they can during their twenties. Those years are going to be the basis on which they build the rest of their careers.

I think that applying yourself very strongly during your twenties will set you up for success throughout the rest of your life.

At some point, people become distracted with raising a family and so forth. You eventually circle back around to some of those skills, experiences, and knowledge that you built in your twenties to help catapult the rest of your career in your forties and fifties.

I would just say to not disregard your twenties as an incredibly important period of learning beyond college.

In terms of seeking promotions, just do your work.

I finally asked, "What do you have to say to someone who finds themselves at mid-career and they are not loving what they're doing?"

I would say to have the courage to do something new that challenges you in a different way or that speaks to your passion.

You should always consider just completely changing jobs at different points in your life. That will make your life seem longer and more interesting.

Have the courage to do something new that challenges you in a different way or that speaks to your passion.

Wendy Johnson
Former President and CEO
Dale Carnegie franchise, Atlanta, GA

I asked Wendy Johnson, "What advice do you have for young women who are just coming into their own, thinking about their careers? Let us talk first about high school girls who are trying to decide whether they should even go to college."

Well, when you are leaving high school and you want to eventually get a good job, it is likely you are going to college. That's the normal transition.

If I were to be candidly honest with girls, or boys even, I think there may be a false sense of security about going to college.

You need to know if you are a person who needs to have this general education. Not everyone benefits from this kind of education, and the costs can be prohibitive. You might be better off picking a skill or a trade and investing in that instead. Invest in training that will get you a job that has specific meaning to you and some potential to move you forward.

> **Not everyone benefits from this kind of education, and the costs can be prohibitive. You might be better off picking a skill or a trade and investing in that instead.**

I know many people say you need a college degree. But I believe there has been a big paradigm shift. There is a huge question now about whether you should pay $50,000 just to be logged on to your computer.

I think the value of the higher education system is up in the air. I really do. But if you are going to college and you have not picked a trade or a specific career goal as part of the process of choosing a college, then you need to participate in the activities at school as much as you can.

Join campus organizations, become a volunteer, be part of something to help others, be a big sister to a freshman or whatever you can, because this is where you start. This is how you learn to be a valuable contributor. That is important. This is also when you start the very beginnings of leadership. This is when you get to *watch* leadership in action, as well.

I think participation in the community or in the school is important. I am a firm believer that what is wrong in our political world today is that we have bypassed the local community. We are leaving it to people who are not creating the kind of community people want to be part of.

For the most part, people who are smart—who have gone to college and who are getting somewhere—are more interested in the national and global world. They have totally forgotten about being *on the ground* in their own communities. *On the ground* in your local community is where everything starts.

Like in marketing, for example, you do not go straight into national advertising. You start local.

> **For the most part, people who are smart...are more interested in the national and global world...*On the ground* in your local community is where everything starts.**

Anyway, I would just say this to those leaving high school: If you go to college, do more than just study there. Get some life skills there, as well.

Then, when you are leaving college, I think it is imperative that you get some kind of training in how to present yourself, how to communicate, and how to build relationships.

Today's younger generation is so screen-oriented. It used to be that the biggest fear, next to death, was public speaking. Now the biggest fear is face-to-face interaction. It is a real serious problem in business.

I next asked Wendy, "What do you suggest to women who are mid-career? Maybe they are not getting where they want to be. Maybe they are not enjoying what they are doing. What do you suggest they should do?"

If they like what they do, but they are stuck in mid-level management and they truly want to move ahead, then they need to get a personal assessment to understand what they are projecting. Maybe find someone in the organization who could be a mentor to them and be honest about how they are being perceived by others in the organization.

Perhaps they are waiting for somebody to tap them and say, "You know what? We like you and we want to move you ahead."

It could merely be that nobody thinks they want to get ahead. Maybe they don't understand that *they've* got to tap somebody and say, "I want to move ahead. What do I need to do to make that happen?" They need to go to their manager and present their goals and their vision for themselves within the organization.

> **[*You've*] got to tap somebody and say, "I want to move ahead. What do I need to do to make that happen?"**

They might find out that they're viewed in such a way that they could never go any further. If that's the case, they need to know that. At this point, they can attend training that develops a professional image to change that perception, or they need to change careers, or change companies. They need to find a place where they will have some kind of a runway.

For those who do not like what they are doing, they need to take an assessment to identify the types of jobs or activities that might be a better match.

Lieutenant General Kathleen M. Gainey
U.S. Army, Retired

Lt. Gen. Kathy Gainey had this to say when I asked her, "For young women who may be about to enter college, how important is it to pick a major in a certain area?"

> Follow something that is important to you and that you *like*. You may be good at it, but not *like* it. It may be important to your family, or to the people around you, but again, you have got to *like* it and you have got to be *good* at it.

> I did all four years of college *knowing* that I wanted to be a teacher, *loving* that I was going to be a teacher. In the end, I taught, but I taught a different group of people than I originally expected.

"What advice do you have for women who are just now beginning to think about positioning themselves for a career?"

College isn't the be-all and end-all. Sometimes it is good to get out, work a year, and then go to college.

> College isn't the be-all and end-all. Sometimes it is good to get out, work a year, and then go to college. Or have what I would call a "break year." Europeans do this very effectively. In Australia and Canada, they have a "gap year."

> Sometimes that year of maturity can help a lot, because you've experienced a little more, you've had a break, and now you're ready to go back and make something happen.

I think it is great to take the opportunity to work in a foreign country, in the Job Corps or something like that, where you have an opportunity to grow and learn. Then, by that time, you start shaping what you think you might want to do in a career.

So, my advice is this: Think of what would enable you to have fun. If you follow your dreams and you have fun at what you are doing, you are going to be good at it. If you're good at it, you're going to get promoted.

Back when I came along, I was told I could be a nurse, a dental hygienist, a secretary, or a teacher. I mean, that was pretty much it. Back then, you did not think beyond that. You were never encouraged to think beyond that.

So, I would just say, "Go for your dreams as they evolve."

If you are in college and you start down one path, but you find, "This is not what I want to do," do not hesitate to go down another path, even if you must go back to school or learn it on the job.

Like me going into the Army. I had totally no background for the military, other than being a military brat. But it didn't hinder me. It actually helped me because I wasn't in a little box thinking of only one solution.

I finally asked General Gainey, "What would you say to that woman in mid-career, who may be feeling stuck?"

Go take that job that makes you feel uncomfortable.

The job you feel queasy in will be the one that will be broadening to you. It will force you out of your comfort zone. It will give you a whole different opportunity, one that you may have never even thought about before.

And take care of people. If you invest in people, they will invest in you. When you learn how to invest in people, then you can learn how to build teams. If you build teams, teams will succeed. You, acting alone, will only partially succeed.

And be yourself. Don't try and be somebody you're not.

If you're not having fun, go find a new job. Life is too short. You will never be good at something you do not enjoy.

If you're not having fun, go find a new job. Life is too short. You will never be good at something you do not enjoy.

REFLECTIONS:

Whether or not you attend (or attended) college, strive to be a lifelong learner. This will help you to continue to grow and gain ever-greater perspective, no matter what stage of life you are in.

Seek to do what you love and love what you do. If you love what you do, you will enjoy your life and you will be the best you can be. You will be a pleasure to be around.

Remember to laugh, no matter how bad things may seem. If you make a mistake, find the humor in it, learn from the experience, and move on to something bigger and better.

Finally, be brave. Say *yes* to opportunities that scare you a little. By doing so, you will learn more. You might even discover something new that you will really love and excel at.

Life is too short not to.

INTROSPECTIONS:

1   Think of three people with whom you could conduct a career-oriented informational interview, to learn more about their businesses and industries.

2   If there is a company or an industry you would like to know more about, but you do not know anyone in that business with whom you could conduct an informational interview, who might be willing to make an introduction for you?

3   If you are not currently doing something you really love, think about what you might enjoy doing instead. Then, think about who you could connect with for an informational interview, to learn more about opportunities within that functional area or industry segment.

4   If you are a parent, what advice would you give your own daughter about preparing for her future career and life journey?

FOURTEEN

Here's Looking at You

The most difficult thing is the decision to act. The rest is merely tenacity.
—AMELIA EARHART

Y ou have finally reached the last chapter in this book, yet this is just the first step on your journey toward what will hopefully become your revved-up rise to executive leadership.

Now that you are aware of a cadre of things that could keep you from executive leadership, perhaps you have come to realize that what is most likely to get in your way is *you*.

If you have had an "ah ha!" epiphany while reading or listening to this book, congratulations! That means you are now more self-aware, which is a very important step on your journey to executive leadership.

Another important key to success is having a clear understanding of where you are right now. Appreciating the reality of your current situation is critical in determining how best to navigate forward. To get started, ask yourself these questions:

- What are your strengths, your passions, your values, and your priorities?
- What about your weaknesses in terms of knowledge, skills, or attitude? Where do you need to put in some work?
- What are you most proud of, in terms of who you are and where you are in your career?
- What might you regret if you do not step beyond your comfort zone to become all that you are capable of?

No one reaches executive leadership alone. So consider how you might begin to build more powerful alliances. Consider who—within and beyond your current sphere of influence—could become an important ally on your journey.

Whenever you have an opportunity to offer your opinion or present your ideas, consider:

- Which stakeholders might be most affected by your ideas?
- What alliances have you already formed?
- Whose cooperation will you need to move your ideas forward?
- Who could block your ideas?
- Who could help you build consensus within and across the various constituencies?
- Who might be a key influencer?
- Who is the ultimate decision-maker?

- What are their priorities?
- How could you help them achieve their goals and objectives?
- How committed are you to seeing your ideas through?
- How committed are you to the success of the overall organization?
- Who is watching out for you and could give you guidance and feedback as you proceed?

Believe it or not, procrastination is one of the most common reasons we fail to achieve our dreams. It is oh-so easy to come up with reasons why we should not take that first most important step forward. The biggest challenge can often be as simple as getting rid of the negative voices inside our head. The reality is, you can accomplish whatever you most desire, provided you think you can, and you act.

Procrastination is one of the most common reasons we fail to achieve our dreams.

As Jodi Berg, PhD, shared, the biggest factor she had to overcome, in terms of accepting the CEO role when it was offered to her, was to acknowledge the fact that she was indeed the best person for the job. When she finally convinced herself that naming anyone else to the top spot might preclude her from achieving her big, bold vision for the company, only then did she say, "Yes, I can do this."

Imagine what the world might lose out on if you do not take that most important first step, and then the next one, and the next one. It is simply up to you to just do it. It is now your turn to say, "Yes, I can do this."

As you progress on your journey, remember you are not in this alone. You might already have many supporters who have your back. You just need to have the courage, and be humble enough, to ask for their help and advice along the way. This is what effective leaders do.

If you need more help than you currently have at your beck and call, I am here for you, too. Connect with me on LinkedIn, or contact me directly, read my blogs, and sign up for my monthly newsletter at www.businessworldrising.com. You can also connect with me at www.heartfeltleadership.com.

If you have not already done so, read or listen to my previous books:
- *The WOW Factor Workplace: How to Create a Best Place to Work Culture*
- *Heartfelt Leadership: How to Capture the Top Spot and Keep on Soaring*

And be sure to read or listen to the sequel to this book, *Strong Suit: Leadership Success Secrets from Women on Top*, in which you will gain even more inspiring insights on how to be the best leader you can be on your way to the top. In *Strong Suit*, you will hear from the very same amazing executive women you have come to know and love in this book.

Finally, keep learning. Love what you do and do what you love. Always maintain a great attitude and never be afraid to laugh at yourself. And finally, be brave and just do it. Maximize your potential. Be the role model you are meant to be.

I look forward to seeing you one day as the woman on top you are destined to become. What a thrill it will be to interview you!

Love what you do and do what you love.

Big hugs and heartfelt best wishes,

Deb

Success just got easier®

About the Author

Deb Boelkes is the award-winning author of *The WOW Factor Workplace: How to Create a Best Place to Work Culture* and *Heartfelt Leadership: How to Capture the Top Spot and Keep on Soaring.*

With 30 years of experience climbing the career ladder within male-dominated Fortune 150 technology firms, Deb knows firsthand the challenges women, in particular, can face in their efforts to reach the top. That's why in 2009 she founded the leadership development firm Business World Rising—originally called Business Women Rising—to accelerate the advancement of high-potential women and men to the top of "Best Place to Work" organizations.

In *The WOW Factor Workplace*, Deb changed our expectations for achieving joy and fulfillment from our jobs. In *Heartfelt*

Leadership, she changed our expectations of those who lead. *Women on Top* will transform the way women pursue their careers and awaken those who believe in them.

Deb speaks to corporations, industry associations, and universities the world over—both on stage and as a podcast guest expert—on career advancement, leadership development, and creating Best Place to Work organizations. She is regularly quoted and featured on radio and in publications ranging from *CNN Business* and *Thrive Global* to *Diversity MBA Magazine, Advancing Women,* and *Hombre.*

Deb has worked with clients as diverse as Experian, Merrill Lynch, Smashbox Cosmetics, Segerstrom Center for the Arts, Toshiba, and Junior Achievement.

Deb received her bachelor's degree in business administration and her MBA in management information systems from the University of Rhode Island. She lives on Amelia Island in northeast Florida with her husband, Chris. Together, they have three grown sons and four granddaughters.

For more information on Deb Boelkes, go to BusinessWorldRising.com.

How to Work with Deb

Deb Boelkes' greatest value lies in inspiring leaders to embody a new kind of leadership style ... one that fosters an inviting and energizing culture and espirit de corps; one that produces and sustains greater employee and customer loyalty; one that consistently delivers a healthy impact on the bottom line ... heartfelt leadership.

Neither heartfelt leadership nor the creation of an engaging Best Place to Work culture can be learned through standard training techniques. Passions must be stirred and inspired. Hearts must be reached. That's what Deb does best.

Deb gives enlightening keynote speeches. She produces eye-opening symposiums, conducts energizing workshops, and consults with executives and high-potential leaders at all levels.

There has never been a better time to take your leadership and your organization to a whole new level ... to a Best Place to Work level ... through heartfelt leadership. Contact Deb today.

Deb Boelkes

FOUNDER, BUSINESS WORLD RISING, LLC

Deb.Boelkes@BWRising.com

Office: +1 (904) 310-9602

DebBoelkes.com | BusinessWorldRising.com

HeartfeltLeadership.com

LinkedIn.com/in/debboelkes/

Other Books in the Series

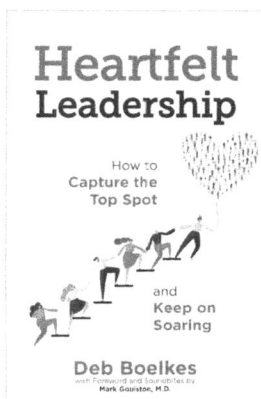

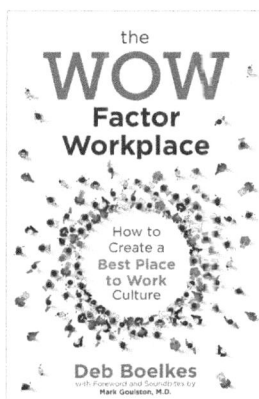

Strong Suit

Leadership Success Secrets from Women on Top

Deb Boelkes

Author of **The WOW Factor Workplace,**
Heartfelt Leadership, and **Women on Top**

Heartfelt Leadership

How to Capture the Top Spot

and Keep on Soaring

Deb Boelkes

with Foreword and Soundbites by
Mark Goulston, M.D.

the WOW Factor Workplace

How to Create a Best Place to Work Culture

Deb Boelkes

with Foreword and Soundbites by
Mark Goulston, M.D.

www.ingramcontent.com/pod-product-compliance
Lightning Source LLC
Chambersburg PA
CBHW071540210326
41597CB00019B/3059